~~EXTRA~~ ORDINARY ADVOCATE:
START WHERE YOU STAND

~~EXTRA~~ ORDINARY ADVOCATE:

Start Where You Stand

Steve Gillis

For we are His workmanship, created in Christ Jesus for good works, which God prepared beforehand, that we should walk in them.

—Ephesians 2:10

CONTENTS

INTRODUCTION

I am an ordinary orphan advocate. It hasn't always been that way. In fact for most of my life, I was simply an orphan observer.

Time and experience have changed me. That's why I am inviting you on this journey of discovery with me. This book exists because I began to grow tired of my inability as a husband, father, and minister to make a significant difference in the lives of orphans. I was living in a fool's paradise, refusing to even accept the idea that my efforts could somehow make an impact in this global crisis.

As a husband, I am a natural protector of my wife. As a father, I am a natural protector of my children. As a minister, I am a natural protector of the people whom God has entrusted me with.

But the question I really had to come to grips with was this: Is it my responsibility to be the protector of children who are not mine, of those without families?

Sadly, I was content to let the most passionate advocates

and nonprofit organizations take the lead. The problem with that attitude was that it was contrary to what Scripture taught me as a believer. I never second-guessed God's heart for the orphan—I just struggled with my role in the crisis.

I wonder if you've ever felt that way.

If you are a tired advocate, an unengaged by-stander, or an overwhelmed church leader, this book will encourage you to see beyond the barriers that often inhibit an effective church orphan care ministry. As Christians, when we look at orphan care challenges from different perspectives, we begin to uncover some of the root problems that hinder our churches from making real progress. If we can recognize these problems and graciously deal with them, then we can begin to make a greater impact in the orphan crisis.

This book offers unique insight and a way forward that will unleash the extraordinary power of the church to do equally extraordinary things. It is a book about seeking new perspectives on an ancient issue. It is also about helping those from whom we may never get a thank-you or an embrace. And it's about using our life experiences and God-given gifts to stand up and do the most we can for the least among us. Courage always begins with the first step. May you, the ordinary advocate, be inspired to take that courageous first step — to start where you stand.

I want to do my part to help transform the way the church cares for orphans. But it's going to take a major shift in the way the church views this issue to make the necessary changes that will bring about radical results.

I hope this book will serve as a spark for you and your church.

Throughout the Bible, God is known as the defender of the fatherless. Our goal as believers should be to reflect the character of God. Right now, in regard to orphan care, many churches look less like defenders and more like lions who are content to sleep in the tall grass twenty hours a day.

Unmatched power lies asleep in the grass.

That pent-up power is waiting to be released in our communities as our churches wake up from their orphan care slumber. Our Heavenly Father's character should inspire us all to take action. But we need to hurry. Spiritually speaking, there is another lion that prowls around, seeking to destroy these children (1 Pet. 5:8). If we don't get to them first, he will.

They are abused. They are scared. They are defenseless. They are sick. They are forgotten. They are prime targets for a powerful enemy.

Look around. That prowling lion is busy wreaking havoc in our communities, while many in our churches carry on day to day in delusive contentment. My hope for you is that by exploring this book, you will begin to have a better understanding of how your church can become part of the solution to the orphan care crisis in your community and around the world.

Thank God for the army of ordinary advocates that He is raising up in every community. It's going to take all of us to advocate for orphans, to lift the veil of our own assumptions, and to allow the light of truth to come shining through.

Regrettably, for the majority of my life I was MIA on the subject of orphan care. My heart has experienced an awakening. I hope this book will also awaken your heart and show you how ordinary people can make an extraordinary difference in the life of a vulnerable child.

—Steve Gillis

Founder | Patch Our Planet

I.
WHEN ORDINARY LIFE STOPS

For I consider that the sufferings of this present time are not worth comparing with the glory that is to be revealed to us.

— Romans 8:18

CHAPTER 1

WHEN SUFFERING CHOOSES YOU

Count it all joy, my brothers, when you meet trials of various kinds, for you know that the testing of your faith produces steadfastness. And let steadfastness have its full effect, that you may be perfect and complete, lacking in nothing.

— James 1:2–4

Suffering is so much easier to deal with from a distance. But sooner or later, it's going to hit close to home—perhaps in the form of a life-altering diagnosis of a relative, the premature death of a friend, the sudden loss of a job, or the discovery of a loved one's dark secret. Throw in a worldwide pandemic, and your life can get turned upside down in a matter of moments.

Suffering is coming, so you had better be prepared.

I encountered a life-changing reality in 2010. June of that year saw me and my family leaving behind the security of a full-time job in order to start a nonprofit ministry called Patch Our Planet. We left the known for the unknown.

Two months later, I walked into a hospital room with a coffee in one hand and a bagel in the other. Our pediatrician was performing a routine exam on our newborn son the morning after his grand entrance into this world. I was excited that my son was finally here. And after a long night, I was also excited to take advantage of the only good refreshments in the hospital—coffee and bagels.

As I entered the room, I winked at my wife, and she smiled back at me (probably trying to woo her way to my coffee). I tried to think of some kind of intelligent-sounding question to ask the doctor—just to make small talk, introduce myself—when he blurted out, "Did you know your son has a cleft palate?"

We sat in silence for a moment, stunned by what the doctor had just said, not fully able to process his words.

We had just spent the night with our son. Everything had appeared to be normal. But at the phrase *cleft palate*, my wife and I could only conjure up images of a cleft lip. We had no idea what a cleft palate looked like.

Our hearts beat rapidly, and our minds raced as the doctor opened our son's mouth. That's when we saw the gaping hole—most of the roof of his mouth was missing.

The full weight of the moment surprised us like a devastating right hook to the chin. Images of future surgeries and life as parents of a special-needs child presented themselves in rapid succession. We were scared to death. The doctor saw our faces and immediately began to backtrack, realizing we had not known—and perhaps that his words may have come out a little too nonchalant.

"It's going to be OK," he encouraged us. "It's just one easy surgery. It's an easy fix. Don't worry."

It wasn't just one surgery. It wasn't an easy fix.

Two strikes against that doctor. I should have handed him my coffee. I think he needed it more than I did.

After a few moments of processing the news, my wife and I made a heartfelt commitment to do whatever was needed to help our son along this uncharted road. I went home that evening to help bring some balance to our three-year-old daughter while my mother-in-law stayed at the hospital with my wife and son.

Around nine o'clock that night, I received a call that my son had stopped breathing and was being rushed to the neonatal intensive care unit. Everyone thought the cleft palate was causing the issue. We would not know for weeks that his airway was being blocked by his tongue because of a condition called Pierre Robin sequence, a connective-tissue disorder. One of the challenges of this disorder was that my son's chin was set back just enough that his tongue would slide back and obstruct his airway, causing him to fight for air and his very life.

That was the beginning of one extremely long week. I slept six hours—total—that week. After giving birth naturally to a ten-pound baby, my wife slept even less than I did during our eight-day hospital stay. We were vigilant, but we were physically and emotionally exhausted.

At the end of the week, we were given the OK to go home, and we quickly found out that our lives were not going back to normal any time soon.

That same evening, my wife began to hemorrhage. We called her doctor and described what was going on.

Her doctor said, "Renee, you need to lie down right now. And if this doesn't stop in the next hour or two, go to the ER. This is something that could kill you."

Here we were, exhausted from not sleeping for a week. Our son was in the other room strapped to an apnea monitor, finally dozing off for a few moments, and we get the news that Renee's life could be in danger too.

We collapsed on our bed and quietly cried until we could finally breathe again. This burden was so overwhelming—and the weight was so crushing—that we could not stand up under it anymore. Fortunately, we avoided the ER, and Renee's symptoms began to improve over time, but the mountain of challenges in our everyday lives seemed to continue to grow.

Having just transitioned out of the security of a full-time job to start a nonprofit ministry, we were hit with the perfect storm.

Suffering chose my family.

Throughout this whole trial with my son, my family was starved for encouragement, the touch of a friend, or even a meal. We desperately wanted our crazy lives to feel normal again. Our family was a huge help, but we missed our friends. We missed our church. We missed life outside of our home. We were stuck in an emergency-filled, solitary environment. And our son's apnea monitor went off 156 times during our first week home. It seemed that our sleep-deprived lives could not become any more challenging.

Since my wife and I were both taking care of our son full time, we were not able to work for a season. We rarely had time to sleep, and we had a three-year-old daughter who also needed our attention. Throughout this ordeal, we longed for encouragement and a connection to the outside world. Unfortunately, those moments were few and far between.

Sadly, and to our surprise, there were many friends we never heard from during our struggle—some in whose support we would have been confident beforehand. After having served as a minister on two church staffs for eleven years, I understood as well as anyone why people stay away during difficult times. They may feel as if they are getting in the way or coming at a bad time.

Either way, for us, many of them just didn't come.

The isolation we experienced during these few months drove me to ask some hard questions. Where do we turn for help when our world falls apart? Would my son even make it if he were born in another country? What if he were laid on the steps of an orphanage and was one among so many?

Through all of the questions, this is what I discovered: suffering is impossible to prepare for. It overwhelms us and catches us by surprise. And depending on where we live, it may even hold us captive.

But it is not to be feared.

In the Bible, the New Testament writer James tells us to "count it all joy, my brothers, when you meet trials of various kinds" (James 1:2–4). Paul, the most prolific writer of the New Testament, tells us to "rejoice in our sufferings" because they produce endurance, character, and hope (Rom. 5:3–5).

And God is right there with us in the midst of every trial.

The Bible says that "the Lord is near to the brokenhearted and saves the crushed in spirit" (Ps. 34:18). It also speaks of our unbreakable relationship with Christ:

> Who shall separate us from the love of Christ? Shall tribulation, or distress, or persecution, or famine, or nakedness, or danger, or sword? As it is written,
>
> "For your sake we are being killed all the day long; we are regarded as sheep to be slaughtered." No, in all these things we are more than conquerors through Him who loved us. For I am sure that neither death nor life, nor angels nor rulers, nor things present nor things to come, nor powers, nor height nor depth, nor anything else in all creation, will be able to separate us from the love of God in Christ Jesus our Lord. (Rom. 8:35–39)

God captured my heart through this experience with my son. I had already started out on a path to figure out the best way to care for orphans. My head was full of solutions. My eyes were full of a vision for how to make a difference. Now my heart was personally engaged to fulfill the calling of God on my life.

You and I may never understand why God would allow us to walk through certain experiences. But we can move ahead with great confidence knowing that "nothing can separate us from the love of God in Christ Jesus our Lord" (Rom. 8:39).

Nothing.

CHAPTER 2

RUNNING FROM SUFFERING

Blessed be the God and Father of our Lord
Jesus Christ, the Father of mercies and God
of all comfort, who comforts us in all our
affliction, so that we may be able to comfort those who are in any affliction, with
the comfort with which we ourselves are
comforted by God.

— 2 Corinthians 1:3–4

It was August 2011. As I sat reading my Bible, I was
reminiscing on what my family had been through the
past year. I came across Psalm 38:10–11 and was struck
by how what I was feeling was an echo of what David had
written over two thousand years ago: "My heart throbs;
my strength fails me, and the light of my eyes—it also

has gone from me. My friends and companions stand aloof from my plague, and my nearest kin stand far off."

These words would change my life. Almost a year after my son was born, I was just starting to have a better understanding of why people had not shown up at our door or called when we so desperately needed to hear their encouraging voices.

People tend to run from suffering.

I know I have. This tendency to run from suffering is something that the church as a whole is burdened with— the church is, after all, made up of people. Our human nature finds it difficult to deal with suffering. It's just hard and extremely inconvenient. We'd rather be at a party or in a stadium full of people excited about some big event.

But what about church leaders? Pastors? Staff members? The ones who are charged with equipping the saints, ministering to the flock, and setting the direction for the church?

Let's look at Luke 10:30–34, a passage often referred to as the parable of the good Samaritan. As Christians, we like to think of ourselves as good Samaritans. But we really need to pay attention to the message that Jesus was trying to convey:

> Jesus replied, "A man was going down from Jerusalem to Jericho, and he fell among robbers, who stripped him and beat him and departed, leaving him half dead. Now by chance a priest was going down that road, and when he saw him he passed by on

the other side. So likewise a Levite, when he came to the place and saw him, passed by on the other side. But a Samaritan, as he journeyed, came to where he was, and when he saw him, he had compassion. He went to him and bound up his wounds, pouring on oil and wine. Then he set him on his own animal and brought him to an inn and took care of him."

Aside from the injured man, there are three main players in this story: the priest, a religious leader; the Levite, a lay ministry associate; and the Samaritan, a hated foreigner. Jesus used this illustration to make a clear point: it's really not about *who you are* or *what you know* but about *what action you take.*

No one, regardless of title or position within the church, is immune from the human inclination to run from suffering. What does this say about the church—laypersons and leaders alike—when it comes to the orphan crisis?

Could the church be guilty of allowing the most passionate advocates and nonprofits to take the lead, as I did? Is the ministry tank too full to even consider starting an orphan ministry? These are questions I continually struggle with. I struggle with them because I have been one of those church leaders.

Before we can even begin to attempt to help children in need, both in our communities and around the world, we need to address this issue of standing instead of running in the face of suffering. The answer, I believe, is not to just dive in haphazardly—we must take one step at a time. We need to know where we are going and how to get there.

At this point, we really need to ask the question, "How did Jesus handle suffering?" We, obviously, need to model our approach after Him. Let's look at a great example in Luke 18:35–43.

In Luke 18:38, a blind beggar yells for Jesus to help him as He passes by on His way to Jericho. The beggar doesn't yell, "Help me! Help me!" He yells, "Have mercy on me!"

What is mercy? According to the *Merriam-Webster Dictionary, mercy* is "compassion or forbearance shown to an offender or subject." This blind beggar asked Jesus to have mercy on his circumstances in verse 39. He called out to one who had power to do what he, in himself, was unable to do.

But then the crowd, those "closest" to Jesus, began to rebuke this blind beggar. They told him to be quiet.

Why would these good-hearted people who loved and followed Jesus ignore such a great need right in front of them? I believe the "church crowd" may have been caught up in "enjoying the show," losing sight of the ones in need of compassion that they were walking right by. Fortunately, Jesus forgives our shortcomings.

Silencing the crowd, Jesus turned to the blind beggar in Luke 18:40–43 and said, "What do you want me to do for you?"—as if He didn't know the answer. The blind beggar responded, "Lord, I want to see." Jesus restored his sight and sent the message that this man's faith had healed him.

Could it be that when God looks to His hands and feet in this world, He sees many in the church responding to these orphans with a demand to be quiet?

Is there too much noise? Too many programs? Do slammed schedules full of good things give us an excuse to not care for the fatherless?

We run from suffering.

Jesus is not surprised by our inclination to run. He understands our human weakness. He knows our nature. He was there when we were knit together in our mothers' wombs. He's also felt the sting of avoidance during His suffering on the cross, as shown in Luke 23:44–49:

> It was now about the sixth hour, and there was darkness over the whole land until the ninth hour, while the sun's light failed. And the curtain of the temple was torn in two. Then Jesus, calling out with a loud voice, said, "Father, into your hands I commit my spirit!" And having said this He breathed His last. Now when the centurion saw what had taken place, he praised God, saying, "Certainly this man was innocent!" And all the crowds that had assembled for this spectacle, when they saw what had taken place, returned home beating their breasts. *And all His acquaintances and the women who had followed Him from Galilee stood at a distance*

watching these things. (Emphasis added)

Did you catch that? Even at the most critical moment in all of history, *humans were still human.* They were afraid. They didn't know what to say or what to do; they were worried that the decision to do something would cost them everything. Even after all the miracles they had seen Jesus perform, they still stood at a distance. Jesus knows exactly how we feel when we are suffering and when our friends have abandoned us. He knows exactly how the orphan feels, crying out for mercy in the dead of night. Not only has Jesus been tempted in every way, but He has led the way in suffering and has shown us that it is actually a necessary part of the Christian life.

We have a calling to follow His example in our churches and a calling to face the fears that may exist on the subject of orphan care, whether these be budgeting fears, resource fears, fears of the unknown, or fears of lacking knowledge on the subject. It is here, in the midst of these fears, that faith—the assurance of things hoped for, the conviction of things not seen (Heb. 11:1)—comes into play in our lives and in our churches. Here—in a position of faith—is the exact place where God is most pleased. It is, after all, impossible to please God without that faith (Heb. 11:6).

In recent years, I've seen the suffering of a child, up close and personal, with my own son. He has come through a very difficult season of life and is now growing and maturing like any other child. Thanks to a lot of prayer, some great doctors, and the full-time commitment of two parents in his first year of life, he's going to be OK. We have his back.

But what about those without parents? Who will speak up for them? Who will help care for them? Who will have their backs?

God has a way of calling out His people and equipping them for the journey ahead. It may not look like we imagined it in the beginning. It certainly did not for me. I would have chosen a much easier route. But if it allows us to return more glory to Him and care for more vulnerable children, would we turn away from that journey?

It is my hope that the church will become the primary place where people care for the orphan and where God's people don't run from suffering but engage in it on some level to bring about hope to those in greatest need. We have to lead the way.

David ran toward Goliath during a battle that was so very lopsided. It looked completely impossible for David to secure a victory. We must do the same thing if we are going to see the mighty blessings of God in the lives of millions of orphans and in the lives of our churches.

One step at a time.

When churches focus their efforts on orphan care problems in their own communities, it does not matter if they only have a few rocks and a sling—or a few loaves of bread and some fish—for resources. God has proven throughout history that He uses the ordinary to display His extraordinary love to this world.

CHAPTER 3
FARSIGHTED RESPONSE

The heart of man plans his way, but the Lord establishes his steps.

— Proverbs 16:9

Have you ever noticed how we constantly place expectations on our futures? We start out as students full of dreams, and our worlds are wide open. As single adults moving through life, we begin to plot out the perfect age when we expect to be married to the perfect mate. When we are married, we begin to think about the perfect time to have a first child. In every stage of life, we seem to be mapping out our preferred futures. Maybe, in some way, that helps bring us a sense of security.

But expectations like these can set us up for a major letdown. Life simply does not bend to our desires or work within our timetables. We discover this as we grow older and move through the seasons of life and experience great disappointments.

It's easy to plan for that perfect future relationship. It's also easy to miss those relationships right around us in the present. It's easy for our churches to grab hold of a big vision around the world and miss the vision that could have been carried out in our own communities. Sadly, our farsighted faith can make the ends of the earth seem more attractive than the ends of our streets. By looking so far in the distance, we may miss the blessings right in front of us.

I grew up playing baseball in one of the most talented baseball communities in America—East Cobb, Georgia. It was from this gifted community that the East Cobb Little League World Series champions came. It was also the place to which parents were moving for their children to receive the best coaching and have the best chance at getting a college scholarship—and maybe even continuing on to play professional ball.

But to me it was just home.

I was fortunate to play for some great coaches and have some good success. My sophomore year in high school, I decided I wanted to transition from community ball to high-school ball in order to begin the process of preparing for college ball. So I tried out for our high-school team.

I knew everyone trying out. Most of them were a year younger than me. And most of them knew me from our community league. I was sure that my spot would be secure.

To my surprise, I didn't make it past the second cut. To put it mildly, I was devastated. The grandiose dream of playing college baseball came to a screeching halt.

Over time, I got out of practice, and my baseball chances slowly began to fade. But my friends began to ask me to play football for our last year in high school. So I obliged.

I was a reluctantly gifted punter. If you don't know what a punter is, look for the skinny guy on fourth down. His uniform will be unblemished as he lines up about fifteen yards from the line of scrimmage, kicks the ball to the moon, and then runs for his life.

Everything went great during football tryouts that year. After months of practice, we finally made it to the fall, and football season was now upon us. I was more than prepared to play—but the first call for punt team in a game went to a friend of mine who was already playing on the defense.

It happened all through the first game, and the second game, and then I found out at the beginning of the third game that I was not going to start again. This seemingly insurmountable wall began to crush my spirit and any hope of accomplishing my future plans of playing college football.

I had had enough.

I walked over to the fence where my dad was watching warm-ups and told him I was quitting the team. My dad listened intently, understanding the agony I was feeling, and then said something to this effect: "You're not going to quit. You're going to work hard, win the position, and then keep it when you get it."

He helped me use my emotions and channel my anger.

I won that position the very next game and played out the season as the starting punter. Still, something happened in me that day that I think parallels what is happening in the church when it comes to orphan care.

Our churches get really excited to follow a big vision. But what happens when that church never realizes its vision or a changing of the guard changes the culture every two years? Do our people just get frustrated and quit like I threatened to do in football?

There is a way to include orphan care in the *culture* of our churches so that the culture doesn't change with every leadership shift. We need to move ahead with practical solutions that are rooted in concrete action so that our people understand how to move forward regardless of obstacles or circumstances.

We all want to change the world. We all want to solve the orphan crisis. I felt the allure of distant orphan care when I first began the ministry of Patch Our Planet. It was evident in my first meeting with my pastor as I was just getting started.

I sat down with my pastor to explain to him my vision to help orphans all over the world.

My presentation was detailed and passionate. I was convinced that I was going to change the world, a million lives at a time. I had plans to radically impact the global orphan crisis.

A friend of mine likes to call this kind of behavior

"passion vomit."[1]

My pastor listened to my presentation about how to solve the global orphan crisis. He asked a few questions. Then, in his loving wisdom and insight, he said, "Steve, don't forget about the vulnerable kids in our own community."

I felt the brakes of my spirit screeching to a halt. I knew what he had just said was 100 percent truth that I needed to receive. In that moment, I realized how far-sighted I was and how ineffective I would be in caring for orphans on my current course.

I was looking to every community in the world as more of a priority than my own. His words stuck with me like the words of my father along the fence at the beginning of that football game.

Truth.

The beautiful thing about life is that when you learn something new, you can adjust. I'm finding a great balance between my passion to see change and the practical steps needed to actually help create change.

Instead of taking our passion for the poor and the orphaned to other parts of the world as a first reaction, let's start at home and work our way out. By doing that, we tend to gather learning experiences that will actually help us in our international work.

A healthy balance—focusing at least as much on your own community as on the international one—is vital to every orphan care vision. Our job as the church is to make sure that vision is clear.

Yet it can always be a challenge to see far off and up

close at the same time.

A few years ago, I noticed my eyes were beginning to not work as well as they used to. I was asked to read a Bible passage in a small group just after I turned forty. In that moment, it became very evident that my vision was changing as I moved my Bible farther and farther away from my face in order to read it.

The good news is that for me and those like me, there are corrective measures we can take. We can purchase glasses, contact lenses, or laser surgery to help us see more clearly.

The good news for our churches is that we can take corrective measures in our orphan care ministries. We can balance the way we approach local and global orphan care. We can limit the frustration of church members by having an orphan care strategy in place that is part of the culture of the church—not just a program that could change every couple of years. And we can take responsibility for vulnerable children in our own communities as a first reaction to helping children in need. It's never too late.

We cannot become blinded by our own passion to help others.

Rather, let your passion help you lead a clearly defined orphan care strategy that prioritizes children in your community first, no matter where in this world you serve. Churches should be responsible for the children in their own communities.

You will find that focus will bring strength and clarity to your global mission as well.

II.
RECOGNIZING
THOSE INVISIBLE
ROADBLOCKS

We put no obstacle in anyone's way, so that no fault may be found with our ministry, but as servants of God we commend ourselves in every way: by great endurance, in afflictions, hardships, calamities, beatings, imprisonments, riots, labors, sleepless nights, hunger...

— 2 Corinthians 6:3–5

CHAPTER 4

THE ELEPHANT IN THE SANCTUARY

And you will know the truth, and the truth will set you free.

—Jesus, John 8:32

I read a phrase that really upset me while I was researching to write this chapter. We've all heard the expression *the elephant in the room*. Wikipedia defines this phrase as "a metaphorical idiom for an obvious truth that is either being ignored or going unaddressed."[2]

But the phrase that bothered me came more from the description of this metaphor. It read like this: "This idiomatic phrase is applicable when a subject is emotionally charged; and *the people who might have spoken up* decide that it is probably best avoided."[2] (Emphasis added)

Did you catch it? You should have because I highlighted

it! What a tragic phrase—"the people who might have spoken up." Imagine how many tragedies could have been avoided in history if people simply had the courage to speak up about that obvious truth.

It saddens me that we, the church, cannot be more open about how our local churches are helping solve this orphan crisis, this tragedy that is at the very heart of our good Father.

And it reminds me of a moment in time when I almost ignored something happening right in front of me.

The year was 1990. The sun beat down on the new brick pavers as I walked the familiar path toward my afternoon college class. My school had recently finished building new walkways around the campus, a welcomed departure from the dirt trails that were the previous mode of student travel.

On this particular day, there were thousands of students walking from one end of the campus to the other in a hurried effort to grab something to eat, make the next class, or meet a friend. I clearly recall that it was the busiest part of the afternoon.

As I was walking, I caught a glimpse of someone who looked like he had fallen off a bench on the new walkway. He was probably two hundred yards away from where I was walking. As my pace quickened, I noticed that he was now rolling under the bench. I knew instinctively that he was probably having some kind of medical issue, one that was really difficult to ignore.

It stood out from the crowd.

I was still a good distance away as I watched literally

hundreds of people just walk by and ignore him. Many would turn away as if they never saw him so that they didn't have to involve themselves in his crisis. People saw the obvious need and did nothing. I hesitated, too, not wanting to be involved.

I didn't know this person. What if this guy died while I was trying to help him? Suddenly, amid the indecision flooding my brain, a switch flipped on, and that hesitation quickly turned into a fire alarm in my soul that called for some response. This was a human being who needed help. *Do something.*

I sped up toward this person as people just kept walking by on the beautiful, new brick pavers. As I drew closer, I was almost at a full sprint when I saw someone else dashing from a different direction toward the guy under the bench. He and I arrived at about the same time. We checked to make sure the guy under the bench could breathe and started calling for help. He was obviously having a seizure. A few minutes went by, and he slowly recovered from this fit that had taken him helplessly to the ground. Fortunately, professional help came seconds after we arrived. The other student responder and I gave each other the "well done" head nod and then went on our way to class after we saw that he was in good hands and was beyond the worst of it.

That day profoundly impacted me—and not because I got a heroic feeling from being a first responder. In my heart, I knew I was a "first ignorer"—that was my first real instinct.

After that event, I began to grapple with questions

that created a lot of anxiety in my heart: Was I responsible for someone else's difficult circumstance? Why did people keep walking by? Why didn't anyone stop and check on this guy having a seizure? Offer some help? Or a bottled water? Anything?

This was just before the days when every student had a cell phone, so people actually had to move and do something to get help. I can't speak for other people's actions that day. I wanted to believe better about myself and others—but I was let down. I was let down by my own hesitation to help and let down by a large group of my peers who chose to let someone suffer alone right in front of them.

I discovered that I have a strong tendency to shy away from areas where I really have no familiarity, like strangers suffering and public seizures. That also became very evident later in my life as I began to be confronted with the giant responsibility of somehow caring for 153 million orphans. Naturally, I shied away from that too.

I've spent over a decade in church ministry, taking mission trips and visiting orphanages. I've spoken about how the body of Christ is to care for orphans, all while having no idea what to do outside of bringing small gifts that fit in a suitcase or playing soccer with the kids. Throw in some face painting and sharing a testimony, maybe even giving thirty dollars a month to the worthiest organization, and that would pretty much sum up my orphan care worldview.

I knew in the deepest part of my soul that there had to be more I could do.

This is a large-scale problem. People tend to feel helpless in their personal responses to something of this magnitude. In turn, churches can carry that same sense of helplessness.

More times than not, I am the guy who is enjoying the new brick pavers in life, refusing to look up to see the suffering going on around me, simply because it is uncomfortable and inconvenient. I would rather look down and stay in my comfortable lane.

I have long known about the magnitude of the worldwide orphan crisis, but it felt distant—so distant that I didn't have to worry about it. I would rationalize that there would always be plenty of loving and capable churches, nonprofits, NGOs, and volunteers who would make a difference in the orphan care arena. I genuinely figured that my support of their cause was enough. So, in essence, I chose to sit out.

I think you would agree that many of our churches are also choosing to sit out.

In some cases, church leaders are not operating in unity and are unable to put together any real orphan care strategy because of the fractures in leadership. Maybe everyone is mad at someone else's leadership or has a personal agenda. Or maybe they are blinded by the busyness of their own programs. I think Satan, the church's enemy, revels in this kind of discord and distraction. The master of distraction would love to have everyone in church staring at the beautiful brick pavers—mad at someone or too busy to respond to the hurt around them. Satan's ecstatic because he knows that when our attention is diverted, it leaves these children vulnerable and unprotected.

Back in 1998, Dean Murphy, a writer from the *Los Angeles Times*, wrote an article about the wild, young elephants of Pilanesberg National Park in South Africa.[3] These transplanted, juvenile elephants were orphaned elephants who were now reaching sexual maturity. They wreaked havoc in the park as they tried to mate with white rhinos, eventually killing some; they charged tourists, killing people and caused chaos wherever they roamed.

Simply put, these animals had no guidance. So the park introduced a half-dozen bulls—mature male elephants—all more than forty years old, from a neighboring park. The zoologists hoped that the introduction of the more mature male elephants would bring some stability to the ill-tempered juveniles.

They were correct in their assumptions.

Early signs of success were seen as the mature elephants seemed to put the younger elephants in their place. Because of this, other parks began doing the same thing. When asked about the success of the program, Markus Hofmeyr of the Madikwe Game Reserve said, "Elephants are highly social and intelligent animals that learn from older and experienced animals throughout their life."

Our churches would benefit from acknowledging their lack of involvement in the lives of orphans. Without the consistent guidance and protection of older, more mature believers, orphans and vulnerable children are also left to their own devices, which leads to destruction and harm.

Imagine with me for a moment what your community would look like if more mature churches began to lead the way in this area. There could be transformation like never seen before in communities all across this world, simply because of the commitment of one church in one community. The spark has to happen before the fire can spread.

Many of us have not represented God's character as a defender of the fatherless. We should get on our knees personally and collectively and ask God to forgive us and then ask Him to use us. We need to acknowledge the elephant in the sanctuary, that truth that has largely gone unaddressed. Then, more importantly, we need to take action.

Only then will we be courageous enough to do something for the millions of children around the world who think they've been forgotten. Only then will we be defenders of the children who are abused by an adult in their lives, afraid to tell anyone for fear of further torment. Only then will we have an opportunity to change the direction of orphans who age out of the system, stealing them away from a potential life of drugs, homelessness, and sex trafficking.

They are out there, in our communities, right now.

There's an elephant in the sanctuary. If we choose not to acknowledge it, we choose to embrace fear. The enemy's laughter will continue to fill the hallways of our local churches. And sadly, the tears of millions of orphans will continue to fall in the alleys, bedrooms, and secret places until we stand up and collectively say, "Enough!"

CHAPTER 5
ASLEEP IN THE LIGHT

> What good is it, my brothers, if someone says he has faith but does not have works? Can that faith save him? If a brother or sister is poorly clothed and lacking in daily food, and one of you says to them, "Go in peace, be warmed and filled," without giving them the things needed for the body, what good is that? So also faith by itself, if it does not have works, is dead.
>
> —James 2:14–17

One hundred and fifty-three million.

That's a general estimate of the number of orphans in our world today. I tend to think of that number in terms of grains of sand or ants in my backyard. I could never count them all, so why count at all? In my mind, I just can't comprehend that number.

I believe *that* is where our problem begins.

We are told that there are more than 153 million orphans in our world. You know how that statistic has made me feel in the past? Like there is absolutely nothing I will ever be able to do to make any significant difference. So what did I do in the past?

Nothing significant.

I continued living to please God, serving others, trying to make a difference daily, and serving God through His church—but I always steered clear of *that* number.

The late Keith Green wrote a song called "Asleep in the Light"[4] that poignantly depicts this mindset:

> The world is sleeping in the dark
> that the church just cannot fight,
> 'cause it's asleep in the light.
>
> How can you be so dead
> when you've been so well fed?
> Jesus rose from the grave,
> and you, you can't even get out of bed.

Although there has been a resurgence in the past few years among churches to tackle the orphan care crisis, the need is so great that the answer can only come when the church as a whole is involved—that's every church in every community.

I am convinced that for the majority of the church, orphan care *is* on the radar. It may even be one of the priorities. But is it part of the culture of the church? Is there an opportunity for the whole church to be involved at some level with support from church leaders? Or is it something that is left to the most passionate volunteer to run?

Let me take you back to my first trip to the Christian Alliance for Orphans 2011 Summit conference. This is the largest orphan care conference in the world. Many of the most passionate and leading orphan care advocates gather each year to exchange best practices and to continue to fuel the orphan care movement in the local church. It was at this gathering that my eyes were opened to the many challenges faced in churches to strategically take on the orphan crisis.

At every turn, passionate church volunteers were excited to share how their churches allowed them to start a foster care or global orphan care ministry—but the church was unable to take the lead in these ministries. So the church encouraged the volunteers to take the lead and run the ministry.

As wonderful as that is, issues such as orphan care need to be a part of the culture of the church. This can only be the case if it is supported in some way by church leaders—not simply delegated to the segment of the church that feels most passionately about it. I write this book as one who has been a church leader and is now an orphan advocate, so I understand the challenges associated with balancing all of the needs and issues that belong in church culture. Even still, the current way of doing things has to change if the church is going to make a difference in the lives of these children.

Even great intentions are meaningless apart from action. I lived in the land of denial for too long. I like to tell people that the reason I am doing what I am doing now is because I have done such poor orphan ministry in the past.

I was OK bringing clothes and toys, playing soccer, painting faces, taking pictures, sharing the gospel, and leaving. I thought that was what orphan ministry was all about. Caretakers commit their lives to caring for these children, and the church sweeps in a couple times a year to give a donation, bring some goodies, share the story of Jesus, and call for decisions.

Unknowingly, I fell asleep in the light of my own comfortable Christianity. Those children did not take even one step toward a forever family on my watch. That thought grieves me still today.

Let's take an important cue from the prophet Amos's message to the Israelites way back in 760 BC. His message went out during Uzziah's reign in Judah and Jeroboam's reign in Israel. It was a time of great prosperity, idolatry, extravagant living, oppression of the poor, spiritual smugness, and immorality (any of this sounding familiar to you?). Amos was a spokesman for God's righteousness and justice. He declared that God was going to judge His unfaithful, disobedient, and covenant-breaking people:

> Woe to those who are at ease in Zion, and
> to those who feel secure on the mountain
> of Samaria, the notable men of the first of
> the nations, to whom the house of Israel

comes! Pass over to Calneh, and see, and from there go to Hamath the great; then go down to Gath of the Philistines. Are you better than these kingdoms? Or is their territory greater than your territory, O you who put far away the day of disaster and bring near the seat of violence? "Woe to those who lie on beds of ivory and stretch themselves out on their couches, and eat lambs from the flock and calves from the midst of the stall, who sing idle songs to the sound of the harp and like David invent for themselves instruments of music, who drink wine in bowls and anoint themselves with the finest oils, but are not grieved over the ruin of Joseph! Therefore they shall now be the first of those who go into exile, and the revelry of those who stretch themselves out shall pass away. (Amos 6:1–7)

These are piercing remarks meant to awaken believers to God's heart. Our striving for personal comforts puts the focus on ourselves and keeps us from grieving over others' situations. It's almost like those comforts numb our souls and deceive us into thinking that because everything is good with us, everything is good with others.

We would do well to take a serious inventory of our hearts to make sure we are aligned with God's heart, asking questions like these: Have I been asleep in the light? Has the cry of the orphan fallen on deaf ears within my comfortable church community? Have I turned my eyes from the sights and sounds of suffering so that my predictable life will not be disrupted? Am I missing out on the greatest blessing of my life because I am afraid?

I think these are all real issues that we, the church, need to honestly wrestle with and overcome.

We may never collectively make the difference that needs to be made until we deal with some of these hurdles. As discussed in the previous chapter, we need more people to talk about the ailing, large elephant in the sanctuary. But we do that with a big dose of grace, understanding the vast needs associated with every church in every community and the current pressures on our church leaders. We are to be God's people who work together for the Kingdom; we are to build up and not tear down.

Can you imagine the impact of the church in the lives of orphans if it, as a whole, would take this responsibility seriously? The years to come would represent thousands, if not millions, of stories of God's amazing grace through His hands and feet, the church.

Romans 13:11 says, "Besides this you know the time, that the hour has come for you to wake from sleep. For salvation is nearer to us now than when we first believed."

Friends, it's past time for us to wake up from our orphan care slumber.

CHAPTER 6

UNINTENDED CONSEQUENCES

An unintended consequence is an effect contrary to what was originally intended (when an intended solution makes a problem worse) that causes reactions opposite to what was anticipated.

—The Law of Unintended Consequences

I stood in the middle of a soccer field nestled in between the beautiful mountains of Costa Rica. The dark clouds threatened rain once again, but the temperature was perfect, and the lush surroundings were something that I attempted to hold onto in my memory. This place was beautiful.

This place was also an orphanage. A few US mission teams from a nearby global conference stopped by in the afternoon to play soccer with the children and to deliver some toys. One team even prepared an evangelistic drama for the kids.

As the soccer game ended, most of the children quickly rushed back to the school that was adjacent to the soccer field. Three children stayed, and the mission team decided to share its drama. When the ten or so youth finished performing for these three children, all under the age of eight, they led them in the sinner's prayer. As you might imagine, they all prayed to receive Christ before sprinting back to the school.

As I watched what was going on, I thought about the lack of priority that had been given to this group of orphans. This was just a stop on the way to somewhere else. It seemed as if the team was more concerned with the response to their drama than they were with the unchanged plight of the children. Why not be concerned about both? This trip planted a seed in my heart that would grow over time and that would lead me to ask, *Can the church do better?*

I was there with another mission team, essentially a part of the same cycle. But as time passed, one question turned into many questions as I continued to reflect on that experience. Why didn't we talk to the orphanage director? What about the school administrators? Could we work with local churches to discover the real needs at the orphanage? How could we help equip global partners to meet those needs long after our team returned home? And how do we help these children find families? Working with the locals is an incredible window of opportunity. After all, local problems demand local solutions.

Many of our Western churches seem to be stuck in a pattern. We send teams to other countries to accomplish a particular task. We build orphanages, paint rooms, restore old appliances, and share the gospel in schools and churches. These teams have, on average, about a week to change that part of the world. And there's a lot of pressure on team members to bring back miraculous reports of all that God accomplished during their time in the field. We all want to give a God-sized report to our donors! Who in their right mind wants to return home to share about the failures of their trip?

There is a real sense of accomplishment in our short-term mission trips to orphanages. Teams experience camaraderie by walking through an experience together. They learn humility. They learn how kind their global partners can be, as team members are served meals and shuttled from place to place. These are all very positive things. But that's short-term ministry at best.

When mission teams receive the greatest blessing, it's backward.

What was really accomplished at the orphanage that day? The students on the team played with the kids for a couple of hours and brought some toys from their hometown. The students from the team cried as they heard the tragic stories of the children who were dropped off at the doorstep of the orphanage. The students sensed the pain of the children. And then the students from the team went home because the trip was over, vowing to come back the next year.

That's the cycle.

What did the students on the team take home with them? All the pictures taken at the orphanage that will serve to remind them of a special place they once visited.

The team received the benefit.

As the students on the team interacted with the children in the orphanage, they developed an emotional connection. When the students on the team returned home, their hearts were warmed at the thought of those experiences.

The team received the benefit again.

The students on the team were humbled after their orphanage experience. They began to compare what they had to what the children in the orphanage had, and they felt a deep sense of gratitude.

Yet again, the team—not the children—received the benefit.

Children in orphanages need us to think about long-term effectiveness. The church's current pattern keeps us from seeing the big picture by prioritizing short-term accomplishments over long-term effectiveness. We have to break our old habits and start a new pattern. There is great benefit to be given, but many are not thinking about the unintended consequences of a short-term *strategy*.

The intended action of many of our short-term mission teams is to share the good news of the gospel with as many people as possible. It is also to accomplish as much as humanly possible within that seven- to ten-day period—and if the schedule allows, to take a trip to an orphanage. These are noble tasks. But couldn't we have a greater impact sharing the gospel by listening to and working with the locals? They can open doors that we cannot.

The unintended consequence of our short-term trips is that teams tend to focus more on the task at hand than on the people and culture they are serving. While we tend to be task-driven people fascinated with books on leadership and growth, in general, most countries do not work on America's speedy timetable, and those countries tend to be more focused on relationships than on tasks.

Our teams should serve our global partners in a way that will create a lasting impact. We should be interested in their ideas, their concerns, and their challenges. We should offer our skills and expertise to serve their visions for orphan care. Global partners sometimes feel as if mission teams from the United States are more concerned with the outcome of the trip than they are with building lasting relationships. Some feel used. Mission teams who do the majority of the work by themselves (building, painting, and renovating) and neglect to work with the local church have missed a great opportunity.

Imagine if our global partners were equipped to help take care of orphans in their own communities. Children would hear and see the gospel at work through the ongoing ministry of the local church. Orphanage directors would no longer feel the burden to tell emotional stories to their foreign guests just to garner support—support they desperately need. These courageous human beings have given up so much to care for children no one else wants to care for. Why should the church leave them out on their own?

At home, we have silently signaled to people in our churches that it is enough to send thirty-five dollars a month to an organization to care for these children. And while it is better to do this than absolutely nothing, it inevitably reinforces the approach of *pray, pay, and stay away.*

Is it the best way to help children find forever families? Let's at least have the courage to ask the question. Ultimately, children are remaining in their institutions. Orphanage directors are burning out. And the unintended consequences of our actions could be having more of an impact than our intended, yet shortsighted, actions have had.

The directors deserve better. The children deserve better.

Have you heard the story of the man near the forest of Gunar in Gujarat? He was boasting to the villagers that there was no need to be scared of lions. In the past he had talked to lions, and whenever they came to their village, he would ask them to leave. One day a lion came to the village, and everyone remembered the old man who was boasting all the time. Now the old man was scared, but he gathered his courage and went with the villagers to the lion.

He saw the lion from a hundred feet away. Slowly and carefully, he walked a few steps toward the lion. He yelled at the lion. He said, "O stupid lion, don't you know this is human society and you are not allowed here? Go away!" The lion simply ignored him. The man took a few more steps toward the lion and again told the lion to leave. The whole village was watching this ordeal. As the man took a step forward, the lion roared. The man suddenly yelled to the villagers. He yelled, "Run! Run! This is a deaf lion!"

Like this man from Gujarat, the church cannot pretend that the orphan care problem is going to go away with mere words. Words alone can make us run from real-life problems, just like this old man running from the lion.

I wonder what would have happened if the whole village would have worked together to solve this problem instead of relying on one man who was just full of empty words.

Our words have consequences. Our actions have consequences. Why not align our words and our actions to benefit orphans with a long-term strategy of care? We are not called to be heroes. We are called to serve as ambassadors of the real hero, God, and to bring Him glory through our efforts. Let our actions be long term and intentionally local in all that we do so that we can advocate effectively on behalf of every orphan.

As one unknown author reminds us, "Snowflakes are one of nature's most fragile things, but just look at what they can do when they stick together."

CHAPTER 7

SUPERHERO
SYNDROME

Overachieve: To achieve success over and
above the standard or expected level

—*Merriam-Webster Dictionary*

My guess is that you instinctively know what I am talking about when I mention the "superhero syndrome." If you have ever been involved in a mission trip, you have seen it played out, although you may not have even recognized it.

"Superhero syndrome" describes people who attempt to create a desperate situation that they can, in turn, resolve. In reality, it is probably a yearning for self-worth.

Early in my Christian walk, my mission fundraising letters were notorious for this type of communication. There was a desperate problem somewhere around the world that I needed to take care of. With the help of my supporters, we could change the course of hundreds—if not millions or billions—of lives.

My support letters were always well intended. Unfortunately, that spirit carried over into my personal life and journey.

My first mission trip was to Jamaica in the early 1990s. I was so excited to go work alongside our team with a church partner there in the heart of Jamaica. I wanted nothing more than to win the heart of Jamaica itself and to share the good news of Jesus with everyone. Clearly, I laid out some pretty high expectations.

What I found when I stepped off the plane was that the Caribbean pace was…slower than I anticipated. Our team spent many hours preparing for this trip so that we could, again, accomplish as much as humanly possible in one week. As we made our way out of the Kingston terminal, it was obvious that we were not in Georgia anymore. We were warmly greeted with blank stares from hundreds of men who were holding these very small, strange-looking things that were half burned and pinched between their sun-soaked fingers.

After our hair-raising, death-defying dirt-road ride through the beautiful mountains of Jamaica, I put our airport experience on the back burner so that I could return to the excitement I felt about helping this small country through our church partnership.

It only took me another couple of hours to once again have an awakening to the speed of the culture. At that point, I knew we had to change our plans, or we would just be frustrated the whole time. I deeply desired to help the poor, share strong ideas, encourage locals, and bring world peace all in one week. I had superhero syndrome.

Like so many others who traveled on short-term mission trips before me, I felt as if I owed it to those who supported me financially to bring back an earth-shaking report of how God used my "superhumanness."

I even went in and out of bars on the street inviting total strangers to come to the meeting that night in the middle of town. That didn't go over too well. People started following me—but they weren't disciples.

That trip was the last time I went anywhere with a false sense of reality. My purpose should have been to serve our Jamaican partners at their pace, getting to know them personally, and establishing some long-term goals together. They would be the ones to carry on the work. But I was so concerned with my God-sized vision that I didn't even ask about theirs. I thought it was the right way to lead.

Thank God for His mercy and guidance in dealing with complete ignorance on fire.

I have taken many trips overseas since that time, including a three-month stint in Argentina. The only reason I have the perspective of our global partners now is because of my experiences overseas and the confirmation of every ministry leader with whom I have had a meaningful relationship. I now realize what Mother Teresa meant when she said, "In this life we cannot always do great things. But we can do small things with great love."

Church after church and organization after

organization in other countries have made it clear how difficult it can be to work with teams from Western churches. They feel they are being used to get to a goal instead of being a part of that goal.

Every country I have been to that is not as wealthy as mine is much stronger in relationships than my country.

I have to ask the question, *Is being an overachiever all that bad?* No. Overachievers play an important role in God's Kingdom. He has uniquely fashioned certain people to work effectively in overdrive. What we have to avoid is the superhero syndrome—our goal should not be to rescue our global partners but to serve them. Good things are bound to happen when instead of talking at our global partners, we talk with them, and listen well.

President Harry S. Truman once said, "It is amazing what you can accomplish if you do not care who gets the credit."

Remember that the most important account you will give will not be to those wonderful people who helped send you overseas. It will be to your Heavenly Father, who called you to serve. Trips will come to an end. But the locals you are working with will still be there in their own community. They don't need a weeklong superhero crusade as much as they need our long-term support, skills, and encouragement.

I think Gary Haugen summed it up perfectly: "The victims of injustice in our world do not need our spasms of passion; they need our long obedience in the same direction—our legs and lungs of endurance; and we need sturdy stores of joy."

CHAPTER 8

AM I WORTH BEING HEARD?

At that time the disciples came to Jesus, saying, "Who is the greatest in the kingdom of heaven?" And calling to Him a child, He put him in the midst of them and said, "Truly, I say to you, unless you turn and become like children, you will never enter the kingdom of heaven. Whoever humbles himself like this child is the greatest in the kingdom of heaven."

— Matthew 18:1–4

Am I worth being heard?

Children ask this question all the time. You may not actually hear the question, but if you are a parent, it will be on display throughout the day, every day.

Let me illustrate.

My home office used to be located in the lower level of our home. That worked out well most of the time.

Short commute. Cheap lunches.

At other times, it was a challenge.

Childcare upstairs. Peanut butter and jelly for lunch. Childcare upstairs. More sandwiches. Did I mention childcare upstairs?

Almost every day I worked from home, I heard the familiar call of "Daddy, Daddy, Daddy, look at me!" from upstairs. There was a door full of windows that separated my office from the upstairs area. It provided a peek in (for the kids) and a peek out (for me). It was a blessing and a curse.

To my wife's credit, she did a great job protecting my work time. But my kids were clever and took full advantage of any little crack in the system.

You just can't stop a child's need for attention.

My kids try to contain it. They are pretty well behaved. But, every now and then, they get beside themselves and need some immediate confirmation from their dad.

Their determination is much like the passion that Dorothy displays in *The Wizard of Oz*—someone is out there who can help her in her journey, and she is not leaving Oz until she gets some acknowledgment from the wizard, the man behind the curtain (or in my children's case, the man behind the door).

Children need to be heard. It is an important part of their overall development. Think about how it feels when you are talking to someone who is not really listening to you or is shifting his or her eyes around like you are not even there. There's an instinctive feeling that the person you are trying to talk to does not respect you or value you when you are not acknowledged.

This is why family is so important for orphans. They need a safe place where they can be guided in their emotions. They need a place where they are valued and heard. The family is God's best and original design.

But today, families are broken, and therefore, children are broken. Although the combined influence of a mother and a father is proven to be the best place for this growth to happen, I want to highlight the influence of a father in the life of a child, mainly because there is such a breakdown of fatherhood in our world.

Every community—and every church—needs its fathers to step up, regardless of their own upbringing and background, to faithfully serve in their God-given role.

Take a look at an interesting excerpt from a *Psychology Today* article:

> How important is the day-to-day presence of a father to children's later educational attainment, economic success, and ability to successfully form and maintain intimate relationships? It turns out that both father presence and father behavior have longstanding influence on children's lives across multiple domains. A research study of school-aged children found children with good relationships with their fathers

had lower incidence of depression, disruptive behavior, and lying. This study also found that boys with involved fathers had fewer school behavior problems and that girls with such fathers had higher self-esteem. Children who live with their fathers have better physical and emotional health, better academic achievement, and lower incidence of drug use and delinquency.[5]

I don't believe that this means that we have to be perfect parents to have our children turn out right. There are parents who have done their best, and their children have chosen to go down a hard road anyway. And I'm not saying that children who grow up without fathers are hopeless. They are not. One other thing that I am not saying is that the mother's role is not important. Moms are crucial. They are a gift from God with incredible influence on their children.

What I am saying is that my response to my children, as their dad, is always critical—and so is yours.

Maybe you feel as if you have missed your chance. Know that there has never been a perfect parent; take a step back and see what you *can* do. We all need guidance and encouragement, even when we are older.

Asking God for help is the first place to start: "If any of you lacks wisdom, let him ask God, who gives generously to all without reproach, and it will be given him" (James 1:5). God hears you when you call.

Let's think about this for a moment. Where will

children without parents get their self-esteem? Who is going to acknowledge their need for attention? How will they know that God, the perfect Father, hears them when they call?

The priority of a family must be at the center of any orphan care strategy. Children don't need institutions. They need families who love and care for them.

When my daughter was two years old, my wife and I rented a small boat at a lake located about twenty minutes from our house. We strapped our daughter into her oversized life jacket and started our journey to the other side of the lake.

We arrived at a beautiful spot in the lake that was a popular place to swim. Since our daughter loved to be in the water, I jumped in and waited for my wife to put her in with me.

She slowly handed my daughter to me in the water. Since the engine was no longer on, this hand-off process made our boat begin to drift.

My daughter turned to see the boat as she recognized her mother's laugh getting farther away, and it sent panic into her whole system.

"Daddy, Daddy, boat, boat, boat!" she started exclaiming.

I tried to explain to her that Mommy would turn the boat around and come quickly to where we were…but I learned that you really can't reason with a two-year-old when she is in panic mode.

So I just tried to get her attention. I asked her to look at me. She tried, but she quickly turned to look at the boat moving away from us.

"Daddy, Daddy, boat, boat…"

I stepped up my efforts by really trying to steal her attention. Finally, she looked in my smiling eyes, and I said to her, "You are fine. You are right here with me. We are having fun. I am not letting you go."

In that moment, my daughter cautiously smiled from ear to ear, as if she really wanted to enjoy being out there, even as she felt the pull of wanting to look back at the boat.

We ended up having so much fun that day. And I learned a lot in that moment.

I learned that you can't rationalize with two-year-olds. I learned that children need to know they are safe. When my daughter looked in my eyes to see if what she was feeling was true, I realized that it was my job to help guide her through her emotions.

This is where the gospel is so central to any orphan care strategy. All children need to know their worth in the eyes of their Creator. And all fatherless children need to know that as they look to the Heavenly Father, He will always be their guide. It is He who is able to do anything. And He cares for them all.

These children need the hope that is offered in Christ. They need His representatives to help guide them through this very difficult journey of life. And parents should be looking into the face of our Savior to get our marching orders, so when our children look into our faces, we can reflect our good Father.

Are they worth being heard?

The obvious answer is *yes*. They are beautiful little humans created in the image of God.

You may not hear them yet, but millions upon millions are asking if they are still worth it. There are really only two choices here.

Ultimately, we'll let them know by our actions or by our silence.

May we all be moved to action.

CHAPTER 9

APATHY, THE OPEN DOOR TO EVIL

And because lawlessness will be increased,
the love of many will grow cold. But the
one who endures to the end will be saved.

— Matthew 24:12–13

If you want to be discouraged, just watch the news for about two minutes. That will give you a dose of discouragement to last the whole week!

The door to evil has been kicked down in our world. We live in a very perilous time, and it can have a paralyzing effect on us. And we can all feel like hiding under our beds and just avoiding all of the pain and evil that exist out there.

But this world needs the light of the gospel more than ever. This world needs representatives of the great

King to share the hope that we all have in Christ Jesus. Remember, "For God did not send His Son into the world to condemn the world, but in order that the world might be saved through Him" (John 3:17).

Therefore, we need to be people of courage and conviction, unafraid of the darkness around us, because "He who is in you is greater than he who is in the world" (1 John 4:4).

My wife, her parents, and my children made a trip down to the old Edison Ford Museum in Fort Myers, Florida, one day as part of a homeschool field trip.

They really enjoyed all of the sights and sounds of yesteryear.

Outside the museum, there was one gigantic tree in full bloom, so my wife decided to step back and take a picture of it. The picture turned out glorious. As she was walking back to join her parents and our children, she noticed a man taking pictures of the tree that our son was standing under.

As she walked by the man, she noticed that he was not taking a picture of the tree but of our son. As you can imagine, this took her off guard.

It only took a few moments for the mama bear to rise up inside of her. As her outrage began to build, she told her parents that she was going to confront that man and ask him to delete the photo of our son. She crossed the street to the gift shop, which he had just entered.

She walked in the door of the gift shop and confronted the man who had a picture of our son on his camera.

She firmly but nervously told this extremely tall and

intimidating man that he had taken pictures of our son and she wanted them deleted. He replied, "No, I did not."

She courageously rebutted and said, "Yes, you did. You show me your pictures, and then I will believe you." His face began to turn red as he reluctantly turned his camera on.

There it was.

My wife asked him to delete that photo. And then she asked him if there were any more. There were a lot more. She boldly stood over his camera as he deleted almost twenty photos of just our son. And then he quickly made for the exit of the gift shop.

You can imagine how hard it was for my five-foot-five wife to confront a large, intimidating man. In some ways, I'm glad I was not there. I'm not sure I would have been so forgiving. I'm hopeful that I would have acted like Jesus—like when He was in the temple cleaning house, I mean: firm but loving.

My wife acted to protect our son, and I am proud of her for her actions, even in the face of fear and the unknown.

Edmund Burke reminds us that "evil triumphs when good men [and women!] do nothing."

What my wife did that day was courageous. She not only protected our child—she stood up for yours.

There is so much apathy in our country and such an incredible amount of political correctness in our culture that it is enough to make the heart sick. When we see someone take a stand for what is right, especially for the most vulnerable, it encourages us to take a stand. Think, for a moment, about how vulnerable and impressionable your kids (or ones in your life) are, and then think about how vulnerable children are in an orphanage or on the streets.

They need an advocate.

Let me take you back to January 2012. I sat at a table in another country with our mission team, a local church partner, and the administrator for this particular government-run orphanage.

We spent time with the children during the morning and then had meetings scheduled with the administrators and orphanage directors later in the afternoon.

Our team found out through our local church partner that these children were being abused in the bathrooms by some of the administrators. We were sitting right across the table from some of the potential abusers. I couldn't take a picture of them and call the authorities. It wouldn't have done any good. I couldn't even speak the language.

But I can help fuel the amazing movement that is happening in that particular country to get these children out of orphanages and into forever families where they can be safe and loved.

I just can't do it fast enough.

My heart breaks with the knowledge of apathetic churches, court systems, fathers, mothers, and political systems that allow evil to go unpunished.

Shame on us for not protecting our children from abusers, molesters, traffickers, and perverts. Children are worth the fight—mine, yours, and the unprotected.

We will never win this fight standing at a distance.

Evil will always exist. And bad people will always have their voices raised.

But my concern is not so much with them as it is with us. There are more of us, yet most of us remain awkwardly silent.

I agree with Martin Luther King Jr. when he said, "In the end, we will remember not the words of our enemies, but the silence of our friends."

Please don't be silent anymore. Stand up with courage and lift your voice—even if that means having to abruptly step out of your comfortable shell at a moment's notice. This is how we will collectively shut the door on apathy and put the wind of change behind our churches to reverse the orphan care status quo.

I know you would agree that children are always worth the fight.

III.
THE POWER OF THE UNIFIED CHURCH

So if there is any encouragement in Christ, any comfort from love, any participation in the Spirit, any affection and sympathy, complete my joy by being of the same mind, having the same love, being in full accord and of one mind. Do nothing from rivalry or conceit, but in humility count others more significant than yourselves.

— Philippians 2:1–3

CHAPTER 10

PASTORS VERSUS ORPHAN ADVOCATES

I appeal to you, brothers, by the name of
our Lord Jesus Christ, that all of you agree,
and that there be no divisions among you,
but that you be united in the same mind
and the same judgment.

— 1 Corinthians 1:10

There is a story line that plays out in meetings and on my phone quite a bit. And it gets me really excited about the great potential that lies—sometimes—dormant in our churches.

The problem is not exciting, but the solution is.

The conversation, usually with a pastor or staff member at a church, goes something like this: "Steve, I'm covered up already. I cannot take on anything else. We have these people in our church who are really passionate about foster care and global orphans. I'm just not sure what to do with them."

Can you hear the stress in his voice?

I certainly can.

My heart goes out to pastors and church leaders. I was one for over a decade until God called me into the orphan care arena. These are my friends and my mentors. I want to do all that I can to help them.

Fortunately, there is a solution.

First, let's all agree that orphan care does not need to be the "banner ministry" at your church. There is simply no way to bring one ministry in front of all of the others to receive the majority of attention. Nor is this what God intends. But it is a vital part of the Great Commission, taking the gospel to the ends of the earth—to every man, woman, *and child.*

Let's also agree that orphan care should be a part of your church in some way, shape, or form. This understanding will bring peace to both sides and allow everyone to work together more effectively.

Most importantly, keep these questions in mind when seeking the desired outcome: What unique role can our church play in our community and within our influence globally to serve orphans? And how can we make orphan care part of the culture of our church?

A Word to Pastors

Most orphan care advocates are not crazy (ha), just super passionate about doing their part to care for orphans.

And it is a good cause. It's actually more than just a cause according to James 1:27. It is at the foundation of pure religion. These advocates simply need support, direction, and an outlet in which to minister. As with anything, many will be able to help, and few will be able to lead. Connect first with the potential leaders. Then try to imagine a day where you no longer have orphan advocates, but a church body committed to serving the fatherless in some way. We should never just leave this responsibility to the nonprofits, governments, or most passionate among us. It's the responsibility of the church as a whole. We should take the lead role as servants of Christ and ambassadors of God's heart. These passionate people in your church will be a great resource for you moving ahead. And, fortunately, every resource exists to help your church establish a custom orphan care strategy that can unify your church around one clear vision.

A Word to Orphan Advocates
Pastors and church leaders don't hate your cause. They actually love children in foster care and orphans around the world. Some have experienced adoption. Many have not. They are usually consumed with marriages, funerals, life-altering counseling, message preparation, and oversight of all the other ministries of the church. The weight of these areas of ministry can be extremely heavy. The thought of taking on yet another cause, even a vital one like yours, could potentially overwhelm them. We expect pastors to lead with excellence in every area of church life. What most of us have forgotten is that God

puts a passion for orphans in our hearts in order to do something with it. Maybe you can be a trusted future leader who can help unleash God's potential in your church. Here is the key for you: find a way to develop the ministry under the church's vision. If you want your church's involvement, start there, and speak with grace and understanding.

A long-term orphan care ministry takes time to build. So don't rush it. You will pay a price down the road if you come out with guns blazing and no real strategy. On the other hand, laying a strong foundation will help your church and the children within your influence for a long time to come. That's what we all want. I like to refer to it as *God's pace.* That's moving forward one step at a time, all the while listening to the voice and direction of God as you proceed.

Orphan care is something that every church can agree on as a priority. Parentless children need families. The challenge is matching the passion of orphan advocates in the church with the vision of the church and its leadership. It can be done. It is being done all over the world. Many have gone before you.

Be encouraged.

God wants to use you and your church to change your community and your world. Take a deep breath. Humble yourself. Think about the Kingdom agenda and not your own.

Then watch God work.

CHAPTER 11

GUILT BY DISSOCIATION

There is therefore now no condemnation
for those who are in Christ Jesus.

— Romans 8:1

It's hard to imagine how to help 153 million orphans. It can be such an enormous cause that most of us would rather not even think about it; deep down, we believe that we can't really have the kind of impact needed to help all of those children.

So many of us choose to think about something else or to pretend that the only reality that exists is our individual reality—in our communities, in our workplaces, and in our neighborhoods. That helps us detach from our inability to help these desperate children all over the world.

In psychology, *dissociation* is a term used to describe an experience of having one's attention and emotions detached from the reality of his or her environment.

I believe that many of our church leaders struggle with the concept of *guilt by dissociation*. What do I mean by this?

First, let me explain that this is not an idea formed out of judgment. I believe that the church is the permanent patch for the orphan crisis and that only by identifying areas that keep our churches from being effective can we truly begin to bring about change. Once we identify a problem, we can begin to implement solutions by defending and empowering those around us.

In a representation of our communities as a whole, many pastors and staff members do not have experience with fostering and adopting. Many have never been to an orphanage or a social-services office. Even as these pastors readily agree that something should be done, this lack of practical experience can produce pastoral guilt and expose a lack of confidence in how to lead an orphan care ministry.

I think these pastors and staff members are worried about leading something that is so complex—that is often foreign to their worlds and experiences. They may fear that if they can't grasp it on a personal level, the church will never realize its potential. Oftentimes, this is where orphan care ministries stall.

Let me give you an example.

Imagine the White House called you today and asked you to speak next week on a panel to explain the science behind near-death experiences. In this example, you are a teacher by trade. You've probably never had a near-death experience, but you are an educator. Feeling rather unprepared, you'd soon make Google your best friend. Or you would fake a major surgery and decline the invitation.

I like to keep that one in my back pocket.

Now, let's say that you have to present—no surgery!— at the White House and that you will be presenting to some very important people. All of these people (who have access to the internet) are waiting for your expertise and will instantly be able to rebuke you if you misspeak in any way.

Pretty intimidating, right?

I think pastors and staff can feel that same type of intimidation when it comes to children in foster care and global orphans. This is a very complex and challenging ministry. Pastors and staff like to be prepared when standing in front of a room full of people. And they sincerely do not want to be seen as hypocritical. Neither do you, and neither do I.

To add to it, the orphan-advocate crowd is so passionate in the church that they sometimes intimidate church leaders in the process. They don't mean to, of course. They just want others to experience what they have experienced and would love for the church to help lead the effort.

This also can unintentionally add to the dissociation of a church leader.

On top of all of that, think again about the pastors or staff members who consider leading the effort, but who have yet to experience foster care or adoption. The concept seems distant to them, and they still have to balance all other areas of ministry in the church. That sets up a very challenging situation in the life of that church.

So how does our church move ahead?

First, we realize that not everyone is called to foster or adopt. But everyone can do something.

That goes for church leaders and church members. We must allow people to pray and ask the Lord what their roles are in all of this. Pastors are not hypocrites for standing in the pulpit to proclaim what the Bible says about caring for orphans and widows. That is their calling. Thank God for pastors. We need them to do that.

Second, we have to bring the passion of those lay orphan advocates together with the vision and leadership of the church. The two can work together as part of the bigger picture in church ministries. At minimum, pastors can share the vision and the biblical mandate of orphan care as the advocates help advance the cause of the ministry.

When this is accomplished, the pastor gets to lead the effort (whether personally fostering or adopting or not), surrounded by the advocates in the church who have banded together for the good of the children in their community. These are people who have come together to use each of their gifts and callings to care for these precious children.

It's what God has called us to do. We work together. We don't put undue pressure or expectations on people. We work in a unified fashion, under the church's vision, as we pray and move ahead with wisdom and excitement.

Henry Ford shared some great wisdom when he said, "Coming together is a beginning. Keeping together is progress. Working together is success."

In this type of environment, children in foster care will win. Global orphans will win. Pastors will win. The church will win. And the community will win.

Watch what happens in your church when your church leaders finally kick the guilt by dissociation and lead the advocates who already exist in the church to work as the body of Christ and care for the most vulnerable.

It's time to remove all the barriers. Great things are ahead for the unified church!

CHAPTER 12

PUTTING AN END TO THE GUT-WRENCHING STORIES OF ORPHANAGE DIRECTORS

And we urge you, brothers, admonish the idle, encourage the fainthearted, help the weak, be patient with them all.

—1 Thessalonians 5:14"

The white-haired orphanage director in Argentina stood before our group and began to tell us the story of one of the little girls in the orphanage. He recalled how she was dropped off at the doorstep of the orphanage at a young age with a note saying this: "Please take care of my little girl."

The director told us that this little girl would stare out of the broken orphanage window for weeks looking for a mother who would never return.

My gut sank. My heart moved into my throat.

This was an experience that generated equally as many questions as it did emotions. Am I doing enough? Am I responsible for what I just heard? How can I help children like her now?

Our team stopped at this orphanage on our way to somewhere else, which is a practice that needs to end. But I share this story here for one reason: I want to eliminate the orphanage director's need to ever share a gut-wrenching story again.

But how do we do this?

There is only one answer: *get the church involved now.*

Let me illustrate.

If churches take the lead to come alongside an orphanage and help the children take a step toward their forever families, the problem is solved. Churches provide loving families, encouragement, resources, hope, accountability, care—and the list goes on. Churches in remote areas, with little or no resources, can act as a trusted global partner to those who are able to come in and help.

If churches are involved with orphans in their communities, directors would have *no need* to tell gut-wrenching stories to visitors in the hopes that these visitors may help financially in some way. When churches participate in an invested way, directors will instead be able to feel a stronger sense of hope and share the stories of positive life change.

Like you and me, orphanage directors would rather be known by their successes than their failures. Let's give them the opportunity by encouraging and modeling support at the local level.

We can do that starting today—even the longest journey begins with one small step. Here are three things your church can do now:

1. Give orphanage directors a break. Cover for them for a few days and send them somewhere to revive themselves for the long haul.

2. Pull together other churches in the community to become the foundation for these orphan ministries by providing resources for them. Get to know the children by name. Be the central connecting point and filter for outside groups.

3. Ask your church to pray about the option of adoption. Every child deserves to grow up in a family, not an institution.

While there are many creative options for getting involved in orphan care, this short list is a great place to kick-start the process.

A friend in a foreign country said to me a couple

of years ago, "For too long, we hosted churches who've performed 'parachute ministry.' They drop in, share the good news of the gospel, and then move on."

Churches in every community owe it to these courageous orphanage directors to provide a strong foundation of support and care until the need for institutionalized care is eliminated because of the church's response to care for the orphan. Prayerfully, that day *will* come.

CHAPTER 13

ORPHAN CARE PLANTING

Let your eyes look directly forward, and
your gaze be straight before you.

— Proverbs 4:25

My pastor likes to create new words; most of the time,
he does so accidentally. But it is hilarious to watch
the creation of a new word during a message. He's right
when he jokingly says that new words and phrases have
to come from somewhere.

So in that spirit, I'm offering up a new phrase: *orphan
care planting*.

Just for fun, the next time you find yourself in a conversation with someone who thinks they know everything,
just tell them that you would love to hear their insight on
orphan care planting.

I think you will enjoy the look on their face. You will be able to enjoy a sip of coffee in silence, even if only for a brief, awkward moment.

Let me explain to you why I love this phrase and why I believe it will help with focus and intentionality. I have been fortunate to serve on some wonderful church staffs over the period of a decade. Much of the overall focus and effort of these churches was given to church planting. I happen to agree that church planting should be one of our highest priorities. We want all people everywhere to hear the good news of the gospel. Church planting helps facilitate the Great Commission. No argument. Lots of love there.

Yet the disconnect between churches and orphan care can sometimes happen right here in this space. And it may just be an issue of priority internal to the church.

Think of a man who is working so hard to get a promotion at work. It is almost all he can see. Other things that are so very important get put to the side in order to accomplish this one goal that he believes will help everything else. It's well intentioned but misaligned.

What often happens in a situation like this is that the man working so hard loses sight of the most important things in his life—his family and faith and time spent outside of work.

I'm not talking about taking the focus *off* of church planting. I'm talking about not allowing other very important things to get left in the dust because we are so focused on that *one* thing. We can do both. We must do both.

Recently, an owl landed on my neighbor's house in the late afternoon. I happened to spot him while I was on the phone outside. So I went in and told my wife and kids. They slowly walked over to our neighbor's house and enjoyed a really close-up view. After I got off of my phone call, I walked over to see the owl too.

I was probably thirty feet away from the house when the owl took off and started flying right at me. I thought about ducking, but the opportunity to see an owl up close and personal eclipsed any sense of being in danger. He flew about a foot over my head. He was flying toward a tree right behind me in an attempt to catch a small bird that was sitting there on a branch. He missed.

We found out during a recent zoo visit that owls and other birds of prey get so locked in on their prey that they lose focus of the things happening in the periphery. That's why they can get hit by vehicles on the road.

I could have grabbed that owl out of midair. That would have been careless, but it does illustrate that owls are hyperfocused on one thing: potential food.

Well-meaning churches can be so focused on one particular ministry that they lose sight of other important ministries.

I use the term *orphan care planting* because it is at the core of a long-term strategy. Churches need to be familiar with the term as it will help them in planning for a long-term strategy for care. So what does it mean?

Orphan care planting is the practice of raising up a sustainable orphan care work and then reproducing those best practices by working through local church networks.

We, the church, should see orphan care all around the world in a different light than we have in the past. As we've discussed, we have settled for traveling overseas with the people from our church on mission trips to "save" orphans by bringing some immediate relief to them (clothing, mosquito nets, shoes, and the like—all good things). Yet we forget to even consider what long-term development would look like in that community. We have to consider both relief and development.

While what we have done has been good, in many cases, it has not been the best. Traditionally churches connected with global orphan ministries have sent teams to be involved about once a year. They spend tens of thousands of dollars getting the team into another country, and the impact usually lasts about as long as the trip.

OK, that was embellished just a little to make a point.

There are plenty of exceptions, I know. But at the heart of the matter, we need to change the way we think about orphan care through the church. Thus, the new intentional term *orphan care planting*.

Think of the orphan work that you are involved with in terms of decades or generations instead of on a trip-to-trip basis. Then work with the locals and create a strategy to care for orphans sustainably and to help children find forever families. After three to five years, consider expanding your team's reach by duplicating the work in a neighboring area—though not everyone on that orphan care team is going to jump at the chance to go somewhere else after pouring their hearts into that particular work and after connecting personally with the children and workers. But at least you have a better opportunity to raise up some leaders who might be willing to go to a new area that is in the same country, culture, and geographic area.

Ideally after a few years, the local church should be so involved in the community that there is no longer a need for your team. On the other hand, given the opportunity, there will be team members who will be ready to re-create the good that has happened in a neighboring orphan work. Build off of that momentum.

Orphan care planting through the local indigenous church is paramount. In the process, we must turn our attention and focus toward adoption. As we will see in later chapters, there is almost nothing that your team can do to have a bigger impact than to help the local indigenous church understand adoption.

These vulnerable children need families. In working with orphanages, keep in mind that you would never want your children to live in an institution permanently. Thank God for orphanages, but let us think of them as a place of transition rather than as a permanent solution. It may be years to get to that goal, but at least the goal is in play.

The bridge from church planting to orphan care planting is not that hard to cross. And we don't have to break one down to build the other. They can and should exist together. We should multiply the reach of our churches and transform our communities by helping care for the most vulnerable. That's transformation on a greater scale.

I would say the same thing about orphan care planting. Don't just transform the orphanage. Transform the community in which it is located. Shoot for the moon. Connect orphans with local churches that will be able to continue the work long after your team is gone. Help orphans take that next step in finding a forever family. That should be your goal—work yourself out of a job! Work within the community to find out who the leaders are and how to get long-term help for this orphan work. Creatively work together with orphan care leaders, church leaders, and others involved to know the names of the children and to have a long-term plan in place for them.

Never sacrifice sustainability for speed. Lasting work takes time.

When we lead the way in a long-term strategy, others are likely to follow. This doesn't mean that we lead like we have in the past twenty years. It means we actually lead as servants, as we have seen in the previous chapters and as we will see in the ones to follow.

The church must strategically think through its orphan care strategy. We need the church to think of orphan care as we do church planting. Take on a mission. Raise up the work. Help children find families. Go do it again at the next place. Do everything you can to help facilitate healthy orphan care work within your area of influence by partnering with local churches and community leaders. Encourage your church-planting church to include long-term orphan care strategies in its leadership training.

It's going to take all of us to make it happen. It's going to take some real, transparent leadership to admit where we have gone wrong in the past and to courageously point us in the right direction for the future.

Let's make sure that everything we do is with purpose. Orphans will benefit. Your church will benefit. And orphan care can now become part of the overall strategy of the church and not just something that is left to the most passionate nonprofit, lay leader, or volunteer.

May we all be a part of the "fruit that abides" (John 15:16).

IV.
CALLING ALL ORDINARY ADVOCATES

A church in the land without the Spirit is rather a curse than a blessing. If you have not the Spirit of God, Christian worker, remember that you stand in somebody else's way; you are a fruitless tree standing where a fruitful tree might grow.

—Charles Spurgeon

CHAPTER 14

GOD'S PLAN A: THE CHURCH

But you are a chosen race, a royal priest-
hood, a holy nation, a people for His own
possession, that you may proclaim the ex-
cellencies of Him who called you out of
darkness into His marvelous light. Once
you were not a people, but now you are
God's people; once you had not received
mercy, but now you have received mercy.
— 1 Peter 2:9–10

My wife and I recently decided that if something cata-
strophic were to happen to us while our children
were still young, we would choose to place our children in
an institution. We spent many hours deliberating over our
many wonderful family members and friends who would
be great options to care for our children, but in the end,

we decided that the best option would be an institution.

That sounds absurd, right? I hope so. It even felt strange to write it. So why do many of us think of that option as being the best option for children around the world who are being raised in institutions? We shouldn't. At the heart of every orphan care ministry, we must make sure that we are working toward the best interests of the child. Fortunately, there is an organization that reflects the love of Christ to these children.

The church is the greatest organization to ever exist. What other organization, ordained by God himself, is located on every corner of this planet? James 1:27 reminds us that the duty of looking after orphans is not the duty of the government. It is the duty of the church. At some point in our past, we abdicated that responsibility, and the product of that misstep has been disastrous. The orphan crisis has accelerated while leadership from the church has dwindled.

The original vision for orphan care is rooted in the heart of a compassionate God. You can see that heart on full display throughout the Old and New Testaments. Can you imagine with me a future where every church in every community is caring for every orphan? That statement may just sound like a vision statement—or a hallucination—but it's the reality of where we could be *if each church assumed responsibility for its own area of influence.* Can you imagine the immediate impact?

It is my hope that churches in every community will respond in a very pragmatic way. Especially in the last decade, the idea of orphan care has been on the radar of most churches, but the actual "doing" part has been a challenge for many. I experienced that myself in church leadership for over a decade. Again, it wasn't that I was doing anything wrong or had bad intentions toward the orphan crisis. Quite the opposite was true. I was focused on taking care of the programs and people that God had entrusted to me within my church. Many of those ministries could quickly become overwhelming to me. So I generally used the secret ministry tool I like to call the "Great Defer," or the "reverse coffee shop treatment" when asked about starting a new work in some other part of the world. Instead of asking, "How can *I* get that started for you?", I would subtly defer with the phrase: "How can I help *you* get that started?" See the difference? That phrase kept me from taking on everyone else's burden and put the ball back in their courts to do something about it.

What I've learned is that if we are going to be the solution, we must be willing to go where we may not have gone before. After all, the church is the permanent patch to the orphan crisis and the best hope for children without families. If we don't act, nothing will change. The church must be the force that moves light into the dark places.

Imagine with me, if you can, a cold, dark room at a remote orphanage in Romania, or think about the child in Sudan whose parents have both died from HIV. How about the child in the US foster system who has lived in twenty-two different homes and has stories that would make a college student blush?

You and I know the reality. We know there are faint sniffles of children who are trying to stifle their cries so that they are not heard. I imagine they are afraid. I wonder if they are abused, hopeless, and hurting.

I wonder if they are dreaming of a nicer institution. Or better facilities. Probably not.

Those faint sniffles are the yearnings of a child wanting someone to love them for who they are. These children cry for someone to defend them. They cry for someone to think they are funny, pretty, or smart. For someone to feel their hearts beating in their chests. Statistically, those sniffles are hardly ever heard by the church crowd.

We have to ask the question, *What is the best hope for these children?*

The answer has always been the local church.

Our friends at Saddleback Church's Orphan Care Initiative call the church the "distribution center of hope in a community." Children receive the best care when the church is at the center of any orphan care strategy. And the church has such a great opportunity to work alongside other organizations and government entities to make sure that children find their way to a forever family.

But we need to dive in wholeheartedly.

Orphan care is not new to the church. God's heart certainly is clear in the Gospels regarding care for orphans. There is no greater message of hope than the message that the church brings. Jesus Christ changes lives and offers eternal life. Every man, woman, and child should have the opportunity to hear the message of God's love.

That's eternal hope. Eternal hope and present hope can go hand in hand. By serving the real needs of orphans in this life with passion and zeal, we work to comfort and bring forever families to children in need. By sharing and showing the greatness of God's message, we work to see children and families come to Christ, allowing Him to change them for the present and for the future.

So you can see that the church is poised to make the biggest difference in the most efficient way.

Any effort that tries to accomplish this massive undertaking outside of the church would be tragic. What good would it be to build a wonderful orphan care ministry without the eternal hope of the gospel? It would only be temporal. As Psalm 127:1 clearly tells us, "Unless the Lord builds the house, those who build it labor in vain. Unless the Lord watches over the city, the watchman stays awake in vain." Let's allow the Lord to build the house and pray for His protection over the city where the work is being done so that our work is not done in vain.

I love the church. It's through this great organization that we will turn the tide in this orphan epidemic. Any effort made to make massive change outside of the influence and support of the local church is destined to end in something short of God's intended best.

We want to see every one of the 153 million orphans in our world cared for and prioritized in the church. If we can't stand up for these children, and we represent the God who is father to the fatherless, then the hard truth is that we are not a good representation of the God we claim to serve and follow.

The challenge now is for the church to move from inaction to action. From passionate coffee shop discussions to practical involvement. From idealism to pragmatism.

From planning to doing.

We're going to make this world bend in our favor and steal back the lives of millions of orphans who think that they have no hope, no future, and no one to advocate on their behalf. No longer. Let the church rise to the occasion today and bring the greatest message of hope this world has ever known.

Will we have to give up some comforts and stretch our faith? Probably. Will it be worth it? You can't even imagine.

I get choked up at almost every Olympic ceremony where the United States has won the gold medal. I love elite competition. I love the Olympics. And I love stories about overcoming obstacles.

I think about the athletes who have won and all that they have given up along the way to reach their goals.

I'm inspired.

I remember a time struggling to embrace one particular gold-medal experience because the broadcasters were talking through the moment. That really bothered me. I was getting angry on behalf of the athlete who had worked his whole life for that moment. He deserved the spotlight—and some silent respect.

I felt like those Olympic broadcasters were hijacking the moment when they should have just been quiet. Their words were not going to make something magical happen.

Sometimes, we do the same thing with Scripture. We elaborate, tell stories, raise our voices, and jump through hoops in order to get our points across. I'm sure they are good points. But sometimes I think it would be better just to remain silent and allow the words to be read and experienced.

Then let God speak.

The never-changing words of Scripture deserve our attention, our silent respect in this moment. These words deserve the spotlight:

- "I will not leave you as orphans; I will come to you." (John 14:18)

- "Religion that is pure and undefiled before God the Father is this: to visit orphans and widows in their affliction, and to keep oneself unstained from the world." (James 1:27)

- "When you gather the grapes of your vineyard, you shall not strip it afterward. It shall be for the sojourner, the fatherless, and the widow." (Deut. 24:21)

- "Thus says the Lord: Do justice and righteousness, and deliver from the hand of the oppressor him who has been robbed. And do no wrong or violence to the resident alien, the fatherless, and the widow, nor shed innocent blood in this place." (Jer. 22:3)

How we care for orphans in our churches is going to vary because people in the body of Christ have different gifts, different abilities, and different callings. That is the beauty of the body.

That is why Scripture has to be the foundation of every orphan care ministry. Through His words, God can illuminate what no other book or strategy can. He will always point you in the right direction.

One of my all-time favorite books is *The Lion, the Witch, and the Wardrobe,* by C. S. Lewis. I love how Lewis describes the unconstrained power of the central character of Aslan, the mighty lion and king of Narnia. He uses Susan, another character, and a talking beaver to reveal the true characteristic of this lion:

> "Aslan is a lion—the Lion—the great Lion."

> "Ooh," said Susan. "I'd thought he was a man. Is he—quite safe? I shall feel rather nervous about meeting a lion."

> "Safe?" said Mr. Beaver. "Who said anything about safe? 'Course he isn't safe. But, he's good. He's the king, I tell you."[6]

Is this the kind of defender you would like to have? Me too. Fortunately for us as believers, we do have that defender. He is good. If you have been looking for a glimmer of hope in your personal mission to help care for orphans, you will find it right here in the very words of God:

- "Do not move an ancient landmark or enter the fields of the fatherless, for their Redeemer is strong; He will plead their cause against you." (Prov. 23:10–11)

- "Give justice to the weak and the fatherless; maintain the right of the afflicted and the destitute." (Ps. 82:3)

- "Father of the fatherless and protector of widows is God in His holy habitation. God settles the solitary in a home; He leads out the prisoners to prosperity, but the rebellious dwell in a parched land." (Ps. 68:5–6)

- "O Lord, You hear the desire of the afflicted; You will strengthen their heart; You will incline Your ear to do justice to the fatherless and the oppressed, so that man who is of the earth may strike terror no more." (Ps. 10:17–18)

- "The Lord watches over the sojourners; He upholds the widow and the fatherless, but the way of the wicked He brings to ruin." (Ps. 146:9)

- "When the ear heard, it called me blessed, and when the eye saw, it approved, because I delivered the poor who cried for help, and the fatherless who had none to help him." (Job 29:11–12)

- "But You do see, for You note mischief and vexation, that You may take it into Your hands; to You the helpless commits himself; You have been the helper of the fatherless." (Ps. 10:14)

God asks His people to take on His characteristics, to defend orphans. He has demonstrated His own character through His word and has shown us how we should act.

If we want to be like Him, we need to act like Him. We may not be mighty kings with the strength and the courage of lions, but we serve a God who is King over all kings, and He calls us to cast out all fears. Don't you think the same God who showed up to defeat a giant named Goliath through a little boy's sling will show up to help you take on a cause that is so near and dear to His heart? I think so.

May there be many "Olympic moments" to come as future foster and adoptive parents stand tearfully grateful and silent at the bedside of a sleeping child they have chosen to be a part of their family. It will be one moment when the silent tears of joy steal the silent tears of fear so pervasive in our world. The light will break through the darkness.

And may every person who chooses to advocate for orphans in some way experience the blessing of pure religion.

Rescuer. Defender. Comforter. Advocate. Protector. That's what we are each called to be.

In God's eyes, there has never been a plan B.

CHAPTER 15

FOR THE SAKE OF CHURCH AND CHILD

Abide in Me, and I in you. As the branch cannot bear fruit by itself, unless it abides in the vine, neither can you, unless you abide in Me. I am the vine; you are the branches. Whoever abides in Me and I in him, he it is that bears much fruit, for apart from Me you can do nothing.

— John 15:4–5

I think we could all agree from the very outset of our discussion that the orphan care system is torn, broken, and weak in many different ways. A broken system does not negate the incredible people in that system who devote themselves day in and day out to care for children in foster care and for orphans globally. Many are heroes of mine. And many are giving sacrificial, Christ-like care. We applaud them. Yet we also desire to strengthen the weak places that are so evident in the orphan care system. We want to build on the many great ideas that exist and come alongside those whose hearts are committed to the benefit of the whole child.

I have never been interested in a quick fix. I'm not interested in a Band-Aid. I want to get to the root of the problem just like you do. To do that, we need a permanent patch. That patch looks a lot like the church. As we have seen in previous chapters, the church is the only organization that is positioned to make the biggest difference this world has ever seen in the shortest amount of time. Some are already engaged. Many are not. But I believe it is not because of unwilling or uncaring hearts. To the contrary, I believe it is a simple but powerful gap that exists between knowing and doing.

I believe in the church. And I believe that with a little nudge, this sleeping giant can become the final answer for children in foster care and orphanages throughout the world. It's already happening in certain corners of our world. We just need to fuel the fire that is already burning and throw a lot of new branches on that fire.

When churches work together, more is accomplished. That is the beauty of church networks of care. If there is one cause that every denomination can agree on, it's caring for vulnerable children. It makes sense to have a working strategy across denominational lines that will engage the church in long-term orphan care solutions.

This doesn't mean that each church has to have the same strategy. As a matter of fact, it's better when each church has its own strategy, a strategy that matches that church's overall vision. This allows for churches in a community to operate autonomously while sharing the strengths of their congregations with the overall community effort. Everyone benefits when this is the case.

Simply following the guidance of the timeless truths of Scripture is the best way to build a lasting foundation for your orphan care ministry. It is, after all, the perfect representation of the heart of God and what He desires for His people.

There is power in the church. There is power in the church *working together.*

All across our country, churches are beginning to cooperate with one another in order to find common solutions to the orphan crisis and to get the gospel to this generation of children.

Throughout the world, churches are cooperating with one another in order to get children into families.

There is no higher calling when it comes to orphan care than sharing the eternal hope of the gospel and working to make sure that every child has a forever family. And that is what we are working toward.

That's what we are asking you to work toward in your community.

Imagine with me for a moment that every church in your community was working together to provide a foster family for every child in need. Now imagine that the winds of adoption begin to blow through your community's churches because of the efforts of church leaders to bring solutions, not just Band-Aids. Now imagine those global communities your church has been working in. Can you see churches working together for the sake of these children?

It can happen.

Again, the good news is that in many places around the world, it is already happening.

Won't you join in the plan that God orchestrated long ago and experience what He is already doing?

We may not live to see a world without orphans, but we can live to see children get out of institutional care and into forever families.

We can see children who were bound for a life of drugs find purpose and meaning.

We can see hope restored in countless lives as we share the gospel in word and in deed.

We can see communities coming together and experiencing the hand of God as they work to care for their most vulnerable.

And we can see the day when the church responds to the faint cries that resound all across this planet. There will be a moment when the darkness of the rooms of abandoned children will be filled with the light of hope, the caring response of the body of Christ.

We can change the direction for many orphans. We can fight for them all. And we'll do it all to give God the glory and for the sake of church and child.

But in order for this to happen, every church needs

to lead. And every church needs a good leader.

Whenever I begin to look for examples of leaders who understand the heart of God, I always seem to start with King David. David is someone who the Bible describes as "a man after God's heart" (Acts 13:22).

Think about the enormity of that statement. The Creator of the universe is pointing out this little shepherd boy as an example for generations to look to as one whose heart was like God's. That's pretty impressive.

Imagine the early years for this future king. Deep, dark silence under the canopy of the stars. Sheep straying off the side of a cliff. Predators stalking him and his sheep. Did I mention silence and a whole lot of time to reflect?

This doesn't seem to be the recipe for a great leader. But God tends to use the most unlikely people to gain greater glory for Himself. And I love that about God's character.

So fast-forward to 2 Samuel 8–9 when David was king, at the top of his game, in the prime of his reign. Things were going well for him in battle and in life. God's hand of blessing seemed to be evident in all of King David's life, despite his deep sorrow over the loss of his best friend, Jonathan.

It's at this time of his life when we picture him contemplating the covenant that he made with Jonathan before he died. They promised one another that no matter what happened to either of them, the victor would take care of the other's family. No harm was to come to them.

So imagine King David sitting on his balcony,

remembering Jonathan, his great friend. All of the sudden, he was reminded of this covenant and wondered if there was anyone left in the house of Saul.

He quickly found out that there was one left. His name was Mephibosheth.

Mephibosheth lost his family in one day. He was an orphan. If it hadn't been for his caretaker, he may not have made it through that fateful day himself. Since that time, he had been in hiding in a small town, fearing his future.

To add to the difficulty, Mephibosheth was lame in both feet. The Bible tells us in 2 Samuel 4:4 that "he was five years old when the news about Saul and Jonathan came from Jezreel, and his nurse took him up and fled, and as she fled in her haste, he fell and became lame. He was absolutely vulnerable and helpless.

And King David sought him.

Because that's what a leader does who has a heart like God's.

King David ordered Mephibosheth to be brought before him. Imagine what was running through Mephibosheth's head when the king's advisor showed up at his house to beckon him to the castle.

He probably thought that his life was coming to an end.

Instead, King David showed incredible mercy toward Mephibosheth for the sake of his relationship with Jonathan.

This is a beautiful picture of the mercy of God in our lives. It gives us a wonderful example of why we should pursue the most vulnerable.

King David did several things in his first meeting with Mephibosheth. He spoke to him as if he mattered. He reminded him of his worth. And he restored his inheritance and placed him at his table.

He went overboard—which is what God does in our lives.

And that's the model that we, as leaders, should be following.

Think of the influence the church has been given. There is still an enormous amount of territory to be taken for the Kingdom. There is more to do than we could accomplish in twenty lifetimes.

And still there remain those who are hiding in those unfamiliar, dirty little towns. Those who have no influence, no power, and no defender.

We have a decision to make.

Are we going to be all right with the way things have always been? Or are we willing to take the time to reflect with God and ask Him what it is He wants us to do? Where He wants us to go?

We need more leaders like King David in our churches.

We have been given much. Our relationship with God has to change us because we have been found. It makes sense that we never forget what our King has done for us.

He's reminded us of our value. He's restored to us our inheritance as His children. He's made a place for us at His table.

That alone should be enough to motivate each of us to go.

For the sake of church and child—let's go!

CHAPTER 16

START WHERE YOU STAND!

Do not wait; the time will never be "just right." Start where you stand, and work with whatever tools you may have at your command, and better tools will be found as you go along.

—George Herbert

In 2010, I launched Patch Our Planet, a nonprofit ministry that exists to help churches develop custom orphan care strategies. In 2010, I had the support of some amazing people and my home church. In 2010, my wife and I had saved enough money to create an emergency fund for several months should the ministry not turn out the way we had hoped it would.

We were not ready for the nine-month hiatus as we

took care of our son. In fact, in the first year of his life, we ran through almost *all* of our savings.

I will never forget the conversation that my wife and I had while we sat on the stairs next to our kitchen. As life around the house seemed to be growing more stable, I told her that I was going to get a job. Our family needed a steady income and solid insurance, especially after what we just walked through. Honestly, I wasn't even thinking about Patch Our Planet being a realistic option.

As we sat on the stairs, and as I began to describe some potential work options, my wife responded simply but confidently: "You need to do what God called you to do."

My hesitant and fearful response was "I know!" We both knew that our momentum (and savings account) were gone with the wind. Time and circumstance had us digging ourselves out of a hole that seemed impossible to overcome. But God had a plan.

I felt an enormous burden to take care of my family. All I could see was what was right in front of me. We needed money and insurance, and I was convinced that I needed to get a well-paying job. We needed stability. But God had a plan.

I knew my wife was right. We needed to trust in God's greater purpose for our lives.

So right on the steps between the kitchen and the hallway, we prayed for God to meet our needs however He saw fit, and then we took a step of faith toward the last thing that He had told us to do. Go and serve the most vulnerable.

Incredibly, my salary was under $7,000 during the

first year of ministry, which we stretched to take care of our family's basic needs. It's amazing what you can do without when you are stretched like that.

Then, seemingly out of nowhere, a phone call came in 2011. I was invited to represent small nonprofits and speak at the White House during National Adoption Month. The Lord began to open doors that had never even entered my mind. From the moment that we prayed on those steps in our house, God has been faithful every step of the way.

Looking back, it's easier to see that God desired my obedience to His call, regardless of our financial situation. We had no idea what the path forward would look like. We only knew that we needed to muster up the courage to take the first step and that He would direct our steps.

I would "work with the tools that I had" and employ the gifts that God had given me to serve the church and vulnerable children.

To be honest, I struggled with all the things that I was *not* able to do. In fact, I struggled for years with a feeling of inadequacy. Then something kind of curious began to happen.

I read Romans 12:3–8 and was reminded of a great and freeing truth:

> For by the grace given to me I say to everyone among you not to think of himself more highly than he ought to think, but to think with sober judgment, each according

to the measure of faith that God has assigned. For as in one body we have many members, *and the members do not all have the same function*, so we, though many, are one body in Christ, and individually members one of another. Having gifts that differ according to the grace given to us, let us use them: if prophecy, in proportion to our faith; if service, in our serving; the one who teaches, in his teaching; the one who exhorts, in his exhortation; the one who contributes, in generosity; the one who leads, with zeal; the one who does acts of mercy, with cheerfulness. (Emphasis added)

First, according to this passage in Romans 12, we are to take a sober look at ourselves, not thinking too highly of ourselves. That's humility. We should be sure to take a personal inventory to make sure that we are serving out of humility and with the proper motives.

God has apparently assigned each of us a measure of faith. We are reminded in this same passage that we are all members of one body but that the body has different functions. We are told that we have differing gifts according to the grace given us, so we are to use them.

This is the beauty of the church.

The truth is—as George Herbert notes in the quote at the beginning of the chapter—the time will never be just right to take a big step of faith. As illustrated in my orphan care journey, the timing rarely felt right, and yet the Lord still provided for every step. I started off working with the gifts the Lord had given me. Taking care of a child with special needs kept our family's full attention for several years. We were not going to jump in and adopt simply because I was serving as an orphan care advocate. Believe me, the temptation was huge, and the burden to not feel like a hypocrite was real.

As the years have passed, our family has found ways to serve vulnerable children and frontline families who have been called to foster and adopt. We reserve the title *extraordinary advocate* for them. We even prayed about and took the first step toward a group of siblings who needed a home. We felt called to take that step. But God closed that door. However, our hearts remain open to His call, and our desire to serve in our areas of strength remain unchanged.

Here's the important lesson that I want to convey: knowing that we are doing exactly what God called us to do, you and I should serve guilt-free. We continue to pray and ask God how He wants our family to respond to the orphan crisis. I believe that same sentiment should be reflected and encouraged throughout the church body.

We are one body with many different parts. Some of the parts will answer the call to foster, some will adopt, and others will wrap around these frontline families or serve overseas. Still others will financially help a family, a child, or a mission team. The opportunities to serve are limitless. And there is great joy when we—as mature believers—can rally around everyone's calling to do what God has called us all to do in this space.

CHAPTER 17

PRACTICAL GUIDE TO A PRAYERFUL STRATEGY

Therefore, since we are surrounded by so great a cloud of witnesses, let us also lay aside every weight, and sin which clings so closely, and let us run with endurance the race that is set before us, looking to Jesus, the founder and perfecter of our faith, who for the joy that was set before Him endured the cross, despising the shame, and is seated at the right hand of the throne of God.

— Hebrews 12:1–2

Over the years, I've had the privilege of fostering many great relationships with orphan care leaders across the world, who have in turn helped equip me in my journey. I continue to grow and add new tools and resources in my life and ministry to help serve vulnerable children and the local church.

What about your church? Your community? Your children in need?

Let's be really honest. Who among us needs to read another book to motivate them, only to have it drowned out by the speed and complexity of life in the very next week? Life gets busy, and most of us tend to forget the things that we've just read anyway as our minds race from one thing to the next.

I've received a lot of encouragement and motivation from many different conferences over the years, but that motivation tends to last about the length of a great movie. Maybe a couple of days. Life never stops happening. What we want to focus on tends to get pushed to the back of the priority list as we chase the tyranny of the most urgent.

We so easily go back to the routine of the tired and weary.

This is what needs to change! People need to feel like there is hope. And you need to know that there are tools available to help guide your church—to help your church discover how it can serve the most vulnerable in the best way possible.

It's time to move forward with great hope and anticipation. It's time for prayerful, practical solutions that will unleash the pent-up care potential in your church.

You need practical solutions that will last. You need something that will carry your church beyond an inspirational meeting and into actual doing. That's why our ministry, Patch Our Planet, developed very practical tools to help every church create a long-term orphan care strategy.

Working one church and one community at a time, I genuinely believe that we will see the day when every church in every community is caring for every orphan. There is a wave coming, and you can help create the ripple of care in your community. In order to do that, you will need resources that will help your church push forward with a united strategy.

My friend Jason Johnson likes to describe a purposeful meeting of advocates as "individual flames that gather together to create a huge blaze." The excitement and momentum build from there.

With that in mind, here is a brief snapshot of Patch Our Planet's orphan care resources that will help your church fan the flame of orphan care.

The first is an interactive workbook for churches called *Let's Build a Custom Orphan Care Strategy for Your Church*. Every church needs a practical guide as they put together or ignite an orphan care ministry. This workbook will make it easier for church leaders and advocates to work together under the church's vision, year after year.

Our interactive workbook will help your team organize its thoughts and ideas as your team plans out the next ten years of orphan care ministry. Too often churches get bogged down because they don't know how to siphon out the most critical ministry opportunities. This guide will help you.

Many churches are chasing so many ministry opportunities that they are stretched beyond their capacities and in turn are not reaching their God-given care potential. This workbook will help church staff, volunteers, and advocates unite under a clear vision that God has placed upon their hearts.

This resource may be the very thing that finally breaks down those invisible barriers that exist in your church, allowing the flood of care to pour out over your community and into the hearts of the most vulnerable.

Our second and third resources consist of our local and global curriculum. These detailed documents are full of principles and best practices that will assist your church in putting together a customized orphan care strategy under your church's vision. These two resources can be a valuable tool to help your church or ministry change the story of children in your community and within your influence globally.

Our local strategy serves a specific purpose.

I have an unwritten rule when meeting with interested church partners for the first time. The rule is this: start by caring for the children in your community first. They need to experience the loving care of a local church. Without a doubt, the experiences gleaned from your local ministry will make your church more effective in its global ministry to orphans and vulnerable children.

In our curriculum for local foster care, you will gather ideas of how to explore, identify, and own a holistic approach to caring for children in foster care in your community. You will also have a flexible road map for your church leaders and orphan advocates to follow from the beginning of the process to the end.

Since every state and every county tends to be unique in its approach to foster care, we've developed some principles that your church can use to create a holistic, long-term foster-care ministry. It's kind of like receiving instructions on how to build a soapbox car. The instruction manual will help with the bones of the project, but you will still have to put your unique touch on it. Because, frankly, there is no one-size-fits-all option in orphan care ministry.

When churches get involved locally, they not only encourage other churches to get involved, but they also help release the great care potential that lies dormant inside other churches. And a focused strategy produces more foster families, more wraparound support, more praying church members, more adoptive families, and many more opportunities to advocate for children who are the most vulnerable in your community.

It's the church rising to the call of the fatherless and to the support of the frontline caregivers—the extraordinary advocates.

In addition, you are inviting every ordinary advocate to pull up a chair at the table and get involved. By not limiting your orphan care ministry to the frontline caregivers, you'll be building an army of support and care based on your church's strengths, serving vulnerable children and broken families with great focus and intentionality. That's what we want!

You can imagine how your community might start

viewing your church as you reach out to serve the most vulnerable. This action rightly reflects the heart of our good Father to a world that desperately needs to know Him and to see His people at work. So whether your church is the county-seat church, the small church plant, or the megachurch in your city, there is a place for your church at the table. Don't ever let the lack of resources deter you from what God has called you to. He will honor your faith step because His heart is for these vulnerable children.

The same is true of your global orphan care ministry.

I met with a church leader in the Atlanta area one time who told me that his church had seven orphan care teams going around the world and that he had no idea what they were trying to accomplish. That's not uncommon. Our hearts can steal all of the attention when it comes to caring for the most vulnerable, especially after having visited a typical rundown orphanage or hearing the tragic stories that follow these children. Of course, we all want to help after that heavy experience. I'm still affected and influenced by those I've served among.

That's why it is so important to have a clear strategy for your global team. The global orphan strategy has to include working with the locals to help them solve their own problems. That is what you will find in Patch Our Planet's global orphan care curriculum.

You will grasp a general understanding of the problems along with some very practical ways to make a difference. You will learn the importance of your global teams and how to put them together. You will be given a framework for how to develop these teams under the church's direction. You will learn everything from dealing with a global partner to training your teams to launching your global ministry at your church.

Your church needs a holistic approach to serving orphans overseas, not just random acts of kindness. And you need to know how you can help a community without hurting the people in it. You will have a good understanding of how to accomplish that with our resource for global orphan care.

You will also find that your global ministry will become so much more effective as you are ministering to the most vulnerable in your own community. Those local experiences will be learning tools that you can carry with you wherever you go.

The great thing about these three strategies is that you have the ability to take them as far as you like. There is flexibility there to adapt to your church's strengths. Remember, God's pace is always the perfect pace.

Maybe you are reading this book as an ordinary advocate who is considering how to bring churches together in your community. Up to this point, you may have felt like David, the young shepherd boy, as he started out caring for sheep in the silent fields. You need to remember that you serve the King and that His heart is bent toward the cry of the orphan. When you call out to Him for His help, you can be assured that He will go ahead of you in that work.

I believe that the ordinary advocate can turn this epidemic upside down and allow the body of Christ to come together for the least of these in every community. You don't need a platform. Time and time again, God has proven that He uses ordinary people to do extraordinary things.

Your step forward may be the very ripple that helps create a wave so strong that the enemy will drown in the momentum of the body of Christ as we join forces to stand for the most vulnerable in our communities and beyond. You can trust the Lord. He will give you what you need as you go. We will turn this epidemic around—one ordinary person, one ordinary church, and one ordinary community at a time.

Visit patchourplanet.org today to find resources to help in your journey, and may God bless your efforts as you start where you stand to become a courageous orphan advocate.

BIBLIOGRAPHY

1. Webb, Josh. *Passion Vomit: Transform Your Passionate Ideas into a Compelling Cause.* Self-published, Amazon Digital Services, 2012.

2. Wikipedia. "Elephant in the Room." Accessed April 22, 2020. https://en.wikipedia.org/w/index. php?title=Elephant_in_the_room&oldid=950666654" https://en.wikipedia.org/w/index.php?title=Elephant_ in_the_room&oldid=950666654 .

3. Murphy, Dean. "South Africa Reins in Its Young Elephants." *Los Angeles Times.* September 18, 1998. https://www.latimes.com/archives/la-xpm-1998-sep-18-mn-24037-story.html.

4. Green, Keith Gordon. "Asleep In The Light." Copyright © 1978 Universal Music - Brentwood Benson Publ. (ASCAP) (adm. at CapitolCMGPublishing.com) All rights reserved. Used by permission.

5. Greenburg, Melanie. "Without You, Dad, I Wouldn't Be the Person I Am Today." *Psychology Today.* June 18, 2011. https://www.psychologytoday. com/us/blog/the-mindful-self-express/201106/ without-you-dad-i-wouldnt-be-the-person-i-am-today.

6. Lewis, C. S. *The Lion, the Witch, and the Wardrobe.* London: Geoffrey Bless, 1950.

www.ingramcontent.com/pod-product-compliance
Lightning Source LLC
Chambersburg PA
CBHW020508040426
42331CB00042BA/94